Harvard Business Review

ON

THE BUSINESS
VALUE OF IT

THE HARVARD BUSINESS REVIEW PAPERBACK SERIES

The series is designed to bring today's managers and professionals the fundamental information they need to stay competitive in a fast-moving world. From the preeminent thinkers whose work has defined an entire field to the rising stars who will redefine the way we think about business, here are the leading minds and landmark ideas that have established the *Harvard Business Review* as required reading for ambitious businesspeople in organizations around the globe.

Other books in the series:

Harvard Business Review on Change

Harvard Business Review on Entrepreneurship

Harvard Business Review on Knowledge Management

Harvard Business Review on Leadership

Harvard Business Review on Managing People

Harvard Business Review on Managing Uncertainty

Harvard Business Review on Measuring Corporate Performance

Harvard Business Review on Nonprofits

Harvard Business Review on Strategies for Growth

Harvard Business Review

ON

THE BUSINESS
VALUE OF IT

A HARVARD BUSINESS REVIEW PAPERBACK

5|19|99 DS

The *Harvard Business Review* articles in this collection are available as individual reprints. Discounts apply to quantity pur-
chases. For information and ordering, please contact Customer
Service, Harvard Business School Publishing, Boston, MA 02163.
Telephone: (617) 496-1449, 8 A.M. to 6 P.M. Eastern Time, Monday through Friday. Fax: (617) 496-1029, 24 hours a day. E-mail:
custserv@hbsp.harvard.edu

Library of Congress Cataloging-in-Publication Data
Harvard business review on business value of IT.
        p.   cm.—(Harvard business review paperback series)
    A collection of articles previously published in the Harvard
business review.
    Includes bibliographical references and index.
    ISBN 0-87584-912-1 (alk. paper)
    1. Information technology.   I. Harvard business review.
II. Title: Business Value of IT.   III. Series.
HD30.2.H376   1999
658.4'038—dc21   98-31400
                                                                    CIP

The paper used in this publication meets the requirements of the
American National Standard for Permanence of Paper for Printed
Library Materials Z39.49-1984.

Contents

Saving IT's Soul: *Human-Centered Information Management* 1
THOMAS H. DAVENPORT

The End of Delegation? *Information Technology and the CEO* 35
PERSPECTIVES FROM THE EDITORS

IT Outsourcing: *Maximize Flexibility and Control* 57
MARY C. LACITY, LESLIE P. WILLCOCKS, AND DAVID F. FEENY

IT Outsourcing: *British Petroleum's Competitive Approach* 83
JOHN CROSS

How Continental Bank Outsourced Its "Crown Jewels" 107
RICHARD L. HUBER

Managing by Wire 131
STEPHAN H. HAECKEL AND RICHARD L. NOLAN

Putting the Enterprise into the Enterprise System 159
THOMAS H. DAVENPORT

Connectivity and Control in the Year 2000 and Beyond 187
INTRODUCTION BY RICHARD L. NOLAN

About the Contributors 223

Index 229

Harvard Business Review

ON

THE BUSINESS
VALUE OF IT

Saving IT's Soul

Human-Centered Information Management

THOMAS H. DAVENPORT

Executive Summary

IT SPECIALISTS OFTEN PROMISE THAT technology will serve as a catalyst for change. They agree that shared databases will allow employees to interact with other departments, creating heretofore unheard of synergies. But, as Thomas Davenport points out, it is a promise that usually goes unfulfilled. IT managers put too much emphasis on hardware and not enough emphasis on the soft science of how people actually share information. Too many managers still believe that, once the right technology is in place, appropriate information sharing will follow.

By contrast, Davenport, who is director of research at Ernst & Young, argues that to achieve its promise IT needs to take a human-centered approach. But implementing such an approach is far more difficult than figuring out which computers work together and how to

1

construct a new network. It means building flexibility and disorder into information systems. It means accepting that different departments frequently can't come up with a shared definition for things that might seem obvious, such as what constitutes a drug, an airport, or a sale. And it means changing corporate behaviors that discourage information sharing.

Looking at companies that have successfully addressed this problem—like Symantec Corporation, Chemical Bank, Hallmark Cards, and Rank Xerox, U.K.—Davenport directly addresses how to rebuild an organization's information culture and how to get beyond the technologies to changing people's behaviors.

INFORMATION TECHNOLOGY HAS A POLARIZING EFFECT ON MANAGERS; it either bedazzles or frightens. Those who are afraid of it shun it, while bedazzled IT departments frequently become prisoners of their own fascination, constructing elaborate technology architectures and enterprise information models to guide systems development. Senior executives who buy into this view promote technology as the key catalyst of business change. But such technocratic solutions

People handle information in myriad ways—from data processing to exchanging E-mail worldwide.

often specify the minutiae of machinery while disregarding how people in organizations actually go about acquiring, sharing, and making use of information. In short, they glorify information technology and ignore human psychology.

It shouldn't surprise anyone that human nature, good and bad, can throw a wrench into the best-laid IT plans, yet technocrats are constantly caught off guard by the "irrational" behavior of "end users." In fact, people who are afraid of information technology may have good reason to feel that way. Companies that ballyhoo their latest management information systems or groupware usually spend little time training employees to use them. Even those who like computers can find themselves hobbled by the rigid structure and rules of many IT shops.

Information managers must begin by thinking about how people use information, not how people use machines.

Obviously, people handle information in any number of ways, from basic data processing to generating sophisticated accounting documents to exchanging informal E-mail messages around the world. For the many diverse information users in large organizations, only one thing is certain: effective information management must begin by thinking about how people use information—not with how people use machines. While it's impossible to account for all the unforeseen consequences of information expansion and use in today's companies, the following three observations exemplify how a human-centered approach to information management contrasts with the standard IT view:

Too many managers still believe that once the right technology is in place, appropriate information sharing will follow.

- *Information evolves in many directions, taking on multiple meanings.* While IT specialists are drawn to common definitions of terms like customer or product, most information doesn't conform to such strict boundaries. Forcing employees to come to one common definition, as some technologies require, only truncates the very conversations and sharing of perspectives that the technology is supposed to ensure. Rather than forcing employees to simplify information so that it will fit into a computer, a human-centered approach to information calls for preserving the rich complexity we prefer in our information diets.

- *People don't share information easily.* Assuming that different departments, professionals, or line workers will want to use technology to share information is one of the biggest mistakes executives make. Yet it is one of the fundamental assumptions made in planning any IT system. That is, if you build it, people will use it.

- *Changing an IT system won't change a company's information culture.* The presence of technology, in and of itself, cannot wholly transform a corporation. Changing a company's information culture requires altering the basic behaviors, attitudes, values, management expectations, and incentives that relate to information. Changing the technology only reinforces the behaviors that already exist. Yet in most companies, many managers still believe that once the right technology is in place, the appropriate information-sharing behavior will inevitably follow.

At one large pharmaceutical company, for example, IT managers tried to implement shared databases and other new technologies to speed up R&D, only to have their efforts foiled by significant cultural barriers. In this case, managers assumed that researchers involved in the development of a drug would pass along all information about it to the people conducting its clinical trial; if researchers had found early on that, say, the drug's effect diminished when taken with certain foods, then patients in the clinical trial could be instructed not to take the drug at meals. Such early release of data, however, rarely happens at this pharmaceutical company. Clinical studies therefore often have to be redone, delaying the drug-approval process sometimes for years.

In this company, management pushed the new databases and software, but researchers were either hostile or apathetic. The IT department was so focused on the technology that they had failed to understand the rigid rules of scientific exploration that govern how scientists think about information. Different departments couldn't agree on what constituted a "drug" or a "clinical trial"—or even what font they should use for research reports. In this case, the rate of technological change far outstripped the pace of change in the culture as a whole. Instead of instituting new technologies, executives should have instituted a program of cultural change to convince highly competitive scientists that they wouldn't be penalized for sharing early and perhaps incomplete results.

Technology, after all, is neither the savior nor archdemon of the information age. At its worst, it distracts and misleads us. But at its best, new systems can support the kind of information use that results in real business change.

What's Wrong with the View from IT?

Since the first business applications of computers in the mid-1950s, planning and control have dominated systems development in large companies. In particular, the concept of "information architecture" has overshadowed a human-centered view of information. IBM created the first structured approach in the 1960s and has defined the field ever since. Originally named "business systems planning" (BSP), later versions came to be called "strategic data planning" and "information architecture."

The analogy to an architectural blueprint, in which the location and uses of different rooms are specified, works as far as it goes. But information architecture was invented to specify computer systems and databases unambiguously. Systems planners believed that information environments could be designed for the entire organization, without reference to particular individuals. Many planners still assume that organizations have a core of invariant pieces of information—such as customers, products, and business transactions—around which key systems can be developed.

This approach has several potential strengths. Such blueprints attempt to structure the sharing of data across multiple computer applications. In addition, since information storage has been a scarce resource until recently, executives hoped that information architecture would help minimize redundant data. And one nontechnical benefit has been widely touted: after a successful planning exercise, executives can supposedly make decisions based on common information.

Most managers don't rely on computer-based information to make decisions.

But information architecture has never achieved its promise. Enterprise models of information types, uses, and responsibilities are too broad and arcane for nontechnical people to comprehend—and they can take years to build. One study of enterprisewide BSP efforts found that few of the systems projects identified in the plans were ever implemented; another concluded that most strategic data plans were shelved without implementation.[1] Given today's rate of business change, even if an enterprise model is finished in a year or two, it's likely to be outdated.

The primary reason for information architecture's failure, however, is that few companies have undertaken such planning with any concern for how people actually use information. (See the insert, "The Information Facts of Life," on page 29.) For one thing, most approaches have addressed only a small fraction of organizations' information—that found on computers. Yet evidence from research conducted since the mid-1960s shows that most managers don't rely on computer-based information to make decisions. The results of these studies are remarkably consistent: managers get two-thirds of their information from face-to-face or telephone conversations; they acquire the remaining third from documents, most of which come from outside the organization and aren't on the computer system.[2]

When technical approaches to information planning are applied broadly, not only do they fail to encompass all of a company's information, they also undercut business change. Rank Xerox U.K., for instance, began a major effort in the late 1980s to redesign its business processes with the help of information architectural techniques and computer-based modeling tools. The idea behind this was that once the new business processes were designed, then the very same models could be used to generate code automatically for a new set of supporting information systems and databases.

After several years, however, a new managing director asked for a simple model that could describe the old and redesigned processes. Not one could be found; all that existed were very detailed data models that reflected the status quo. The technicians had lost the objective of business change in the details of modeling. Now Rank Xerox uses simpler approaches to do process modeling, such as flow charts and cost buildup charts, and has made some successful changes; for example, it has saved $11 million annually in sales-order processing by eliminating approval steps and better integrating the sales force with the entire order-management process. Now the company uses information architecture only to design specific systems.

As at Rank Xerox and other large companies, information architects have assumed that common information is created through the development of a computer model instead of through the long and often arduous process of reaching a shared understanding. They haven't identified, trained, or monitored the desired behaviors for information users and providers, both of whom must cooperate if common information is to be developed. Most important, they make the unrealistic assumption that most of a company's information can be organized according to a few common terms.

A Natural Mess: Multiple Information Meanings

While information architecture can't capture the reality of human behavior, the alternative is hard for traditional managers to grasp. That's because a human-centered approach assumes information is complex, ever-expanding, and impossible to control completely. The natural world is a more apt metaphor for the information age than architecture. From this holistic perspective, all information doesn't have to be common; some disorder and even redundancy may be desirable. (See the chart, "Human-Centered IT Managers Focus on How People Use Information Rather than Machines.")

No matter how simple or basic a unit of information may seem, there can be valid disagreements about its meaning. At Digital Equipment Corporation, for example, a "sale" to the indirect marketing organization happened when a distributor or reseller ordered a computer; but to direct marketing, the sale occurred only when the end customer took delivery. Even within direct marketing, there were differences of opinion: salespeople recorded a sale when the order was placed, manufacturing and logistics when the product was delivered, and finance when it was paid for.

Human-Centered IT Managers Focus on How People Use Information Rather than Machines

Information architectures:	Human-centered approaches:
Focus on computerized data	Focus on broad information types
Emphasize information provision	Emphasize information use and sharing
Assume permanence of solutions	Assume transience of solutions
Assume single meaning of terms	Assume multiple meanings of terms
Stop when design is done or when system is built	Continue until desired behavior is achieved enterprisewide
Build enterprisewide structures	Build point-specific structures
Assume compliance with policies	Assume compliance is gained over time through influence
Control users' information environments	Let individuals design their own information environments

At American Airlines, there are several perspectives on what an "airport" is. Some managers argue that an airport is any location to which American has scheduled service; others count any airport granted that status by the international standards body. At Union Pacific Railroad, there's little consensus on what a "train" is. Is it a locomotive, all cars actually pulled from an origin to a destination, or an abstract scheduling entity? Even U.S. Department of Agriculture officials can't agree on the meaning of "farm."

No unit of information is too basic to prevent disagreement about its meaning: USDA officials can't even agree on what a farm is.

These multiple meanings make the job of information management treacherous at best. At one oil exploration company, for example, information architects worked for years on ineffective models because people assigned different meanings to "oil location." Some users defined it as the original geographic coordinates in the ground; others thought it was the well from which oil sprang; still others used the term to refer to the oil's current location in a tank farm or pipeline. Each definition found its way into computer databases. As a result, it was difficult to share even the most basic information on the production of different sites. Among many other problems, the company couldn't accurately monitor the performance of specific wells or figure the taxes it owed states and counties where the oil was pumped.

In this case, the CEO finally dictated to the entire management team what "oil location" would henceforth mean: an official corporate algorithm that reflected drilling location, well angle, and drill depth. Those managers or other employees who used alternative meanings would lose their jobs. Although this solution is extreme, it did achieve the desired result: consensus on the meaning of oil location and better information on production that could be shared.

But while multiple meanings can create problems for organizational integration and information sharing, they shouldn't always be eliminated, especially in large companies with diverse businesses. In fact, given the importance of information to the success of individuals and groups within organizations, managers should expect pressures to define information in ways that are useful to these smaller units. There will always be a healthy tension between *information globalism*, which seeks to create meanings that apply to an entire organization, and *information particularism*, in which individuals and small groups define information in ways that make sense to them.

Another large computer company exemplifies the natural tension between particularism and globalism. This company is renowned for granting autonomy to product and geographical units. That autonomy extends to information; when it comes to financial information, for example, there are 103 general ledgers. Divisional, geographical, and product executives can therefore count costs, revenues, and profits in ways that are most meaningful for their particular products or businesses. To deal with aggregation, this company maintains a corporate-level ledger to consolidate results across common financial categories.

Undoubtedly, such particularism turns aggregation and information sharing into a challenge. Even though there is a corporate-level information stream, managers are often evaluated by comparing their financial results against that corporate stream. Much effort goes into reconciling and explaining how the local stream relates to the corporate stream. Finance managers keep trying to remove as many entries from ledgers as possible and coaxing local executives into using corporate-level information when they can. Some top managers are actively trying to get rid of the local ledgers altogether. But while dual information streams are messy and hard to control, they seem realistic for this diverse company.

A larger managerial barrier, however, remains: operating with multiple meanings also requires basic changes in behavior—not only for information providers, who categorize and collect the information, but also for users. The CEO who is annoyed when told there's no quick answer to how many customers (or employees or products) the company has is just as guilty of oversimplifying information as the database designer who insists on one definition of customer.

And when it *is* necessary to define common meanings, the process requires much more management participation and time than many assume or want to allot. For instance, Xerox did data modeling and administration for 20 years, but in the words of the director of information management, "We got nowhere." These initiatives were driven by IT rather than by senior business managers; they were always abandoned in favor of specific development projects like the new order-processing or billing system, which yielded obvious benefits.

Finally, Xerox's IT department asked senior executives to identify the key pieces of information on which the entire business should be run. The executives debated the issue on several occasions but weren't able to reach a consensus. They did agree, however, that their main priorities were customer, financial, and product information—in that order.

Xerox's IT department then took another tack. From around the world, 15 marketing and sales managers, accompanied by their IT counterparts, met to agree on the set of common customer information the company would use. As usual, people disagreed about what "customer" meant. But these managers eventually agreed to define customers as corporations that had already purchased products or services from Xerox and to refer to them with a common worldwide number; they also reached consensus on 11 other customer-oriented terms, including customer-satisfaction measures. This coordinated approach allowed country managers to then create customer information that the IT department has now combined into a global data warehouse.

The Trouble with Information Sharing

In today's competitive business environment, it makes sense to give information particularism its due; but as Xerox's experience with customer information illustrates, executives must also decide which aspects of a company's information are global. More to the point, executives must determine how such information is to be shared effectively—one of the trickiest management issues for today's companies.

Paranoia about dissemination has its roots in practical information issues.

While information architecture can specify who controls information, such rigid models don't account for the unpredictable growth of information or human nature.

Some managers are quick to point out the obvious difficulties with information sharing, especially when it's driven by new technologies like electronic mail. If sharing makes it easier for a company's employees to get at critical information, it also opens the way for any interested external parties—competitors, attorneys, even computer hackers. Given the many recent and highly visible cases of departing employees allegedly taking with them reams (or diskettes) of proprietary information, many executives wonder whether or not such information should be widely disseminated in the first place.

Paranoia about external opportunists has its roots in practical information issues. For information to be shared, it must first be structured and compiled, which makes it easier to steal or subpoena. For example, when Otis Elevator began to compile information on elevator reliability and performance—which would enable sharing among managers, service personnel, and new product designers—the company's internal counsel feared having to produce this information if the company were sued for an elevator-related accident. This hasn't happened so far, but it's all too easy to understand this attorney's concerns. Ironically, his response exposes some of the old-line corporate attitudes about controlling information through secrecy and ambiguity.

When Chemical Bank and Manufacturers Hanover merged, two information cultures clashed.

Indeed, the internal problems that arise with information sharing have the most impact on companies and are much less obvious than external thieves and ex-employees with a grudge. Mergers produce some of the most visible clashes, since managers from companies with sometimes very different attitudes toward information use often find themselves thrown together. For example, a number of contentious issues surfaced at

Chemical Bank shortly after it merged with Manufacturers Hanover.

The two banks had very different information cultures. Chemical Bank favored sharing information
across departments and product groups. Manufacturers
Hanover believed that each group owned its information
and could choose not to share it. To help integrate banking operations, senior executives decided to create a
basic set of information management principles, a process that allowed managers of both banks to discuss
which policy should prevail.

One draft principle stated that if a business area had
a legitimate need for information, it should get it. But
managers from the different banks first disagreed about
access to sensitive information—would they be breach-
ing both customer security and trust? And what was a
"legitimate need," anyway? For instance, should the private banking group furnish information on wealthy customers to the capital markets division, which could then
promote a bond offering to them? If so, which of the
groups were responsible for identifying likely prospects,
notifying the appropriate managers, and outputting the
customer information in the correct format for the capital markets division?

Other Chemical Bank principles addressed the need
for a clear owner for each major piece of information
and clarified responsibilities and priorities for supplying
information to other parts of the bank. These information management principles aren't magic, but they've
hastened the integration of the two banks and limited
disagreements about important information issues. As
with so many human-centered information management techniques, the process of developing principles—
of hammering out how information is defined and distributed—was more important than any fixed result.

In this case, bank executives were well aware of what made information sharing such a touchy subject. But consider a less successful example: the IT managers of a large telecommunications company generated an admirable set of their own information management principles. They addressed the need to establish "enterprise information" and the ways such corporate information should be managed and shared. But while corporate senior managers reviewed these principles, divisional heads weren't consulted. As a result, several divisions decided they were separate "enterprises" and could therefore define their own information.

Such natural power plays, malicious or not, are legion. The will to power—whether that applies to CEOs, separate divisions, line supervisors, or individual professionals—is the main reason why new information technologies don't inevitably lead to flattened hierarchies and empowered employees. Working out information issues in a company with a monolithic culture—instead of wrestling with two competing information cultures that result from a merger—often involves digging out entrenched attitudes toward organizational control.

In such companies, technologies that promote information sharing can end up controlling employees rather than empowering them. When lower level workers are ordered to "share" information with those higher up the corporate ladder, a cutthroat information culture of meddling micro-management can result. At the refining and marketing division of a large oil company, for example, the division president delighted in being able to use his computer to peer electronically over the shoulders of oil traders—and occasionally to override or initiate a deal.

On the other hand, Xerox's executive support system has been limited to accessing data two levels below the user—precisely to avoid this type of excessive control. Such human-centered technology implementations are still rare, but they indicate the way managers must think about the issues that information sharing brings to the surface.

Populist exhortations to the contrary, unlimited information sharing doesn't work. In fact, increased information sharing can either improve or actively harm company morale. Sharing information about actual corporate performance is usually good for morale—even when performance is poor, since uninformed

Many people suffer from far too much noninformation rather than the "information overload" they complain about.

employees often assume that it's worse than it really is. Sharing rumors, however, can be demoralizing.

An information systems manager at a New York bank, for example, created a Lotus Notes bulletin board that he called the "Rumor Mill." The system allowed employees in his department to share rumors easily; the manager could then quash false ones on-line. This experiment worked just fine—until rumors were posted about the manager's own departure from the bank. When he refused to comment, employees correctly surmised it was true. They became cynical about this attempt to share information through technology, since the manager hadn't communicated with them on this particular piece of information. Needless to say, Rumor Mill was not continued by his successor.

Sharing rumors in this fashion underscores the distinction between information and *noninformation*. Many people suffer from far too much noninformation—which companies seem to generate with ease and at the

expense of useful information—rather than the "information overload" they complain about. Any heavy E-
mail user can testify to the junk mail problem. Right
now I have more than 160 messages in my electronic
mailbox, some of which inform me that one colleague
lost his appointment book or that another wanted to be
included in last Thursday's pizza run. I should never
have received them, and now I don't have the time to
delete them.

Technologists are working on personalized filters or
"agents" that can separate real information from junk.
But it's likely that good marketers of electronic information will find ways to circumvent filters—just as direct
mail now looks like a tax refund or personal check. In
fact, some communication technologies just exacerbate
this problem.

At Tandem Computers, for example, a combination
E-mail/bulletin board allows field-service personnel to
send a "has anyone seen this problem?" message to all
technical people in the company. The service technician
may get an answer, but is it really necessary for everyone
to read this message? As in so many other cases, simply
implementing an electronic-mail system—without any
guidelines for how to use it—won't resolve the complicated issues of information sharing and management.

If some companies generate noninformation through
E-mail, others rely on it too much to communicate real
information. Although such technologies can improve
organizational communications, they have their limits.
Several researchers have argued persuasively that the organizational trust and interpersonal context necessary to
achieve a true network organization aren't based solely
on electronic networks.[3] Rather, relationships must be
initially constructed through face-to-face meetings.

Symantec Corporation, for instance, found that electronic mail is not all it's cracked up to be. At Symantec, a California software company that grew rapidly through acquisition and ended up with relatively autonomous product groups, there was substantial use of electronic mail. Indeed, senior executives believed E-mail was the fastest way to forge connections in this virtual corporation. But senior managers soon realized their diverse organization still didn't communicate very well. They concluded that people in geographically far-flung product groups just didn't see each other enough.

To address the problem, executives organized the first companywide meeting. Managers began communicating about important issues through several different routes: letters to employees' homes, face-to-face conversations, as well as E-mail memos. In some cases, they made the same announcement across all media to make sure all employees heard essential news. The company's executives noticed substantial improvement in the problem thereafter; employees complained less about communication problems, and those in the field talked about Symantec's overall strategic directions with greater understanding.

New communication technologies will certainly support information sharing when physical proximity isn't a possibility. But as Symantec's story shows, the proliferation of these technologies has created a new problem: how to choose among all the alternatives. A sales rep who wants to communicate with a customer can use first-class mail, express mail, voice mail, electronic mail,

Changing the company's information culture is the best way to implement IT, but it's also the hardest to carry out.

a fax, an electronic bulletin board, videoconferencing, or the telephone—not to mention a face-to-face meeting.

Few of us have a clear sense of which alternative is most appropriate for a given communication. But while using a suboptimal medium is not yet a corporate crime, managers should at least acknowledge the confusion. And regardless of the technical form of communication, managers must bear in mind that employees who work together still need regular personal contact.

Preparing the Cultural Ground for IT

If companies as diverse as Symantec, Chemical Bank, Xerox—even the oil company with the controlling division president—are all struggling with information-sharing problems, it's because such issues are unavoidable in today's global economy. What many have discovered, however, is that their solutions do not turn out to be particularly "scientific." Indeed, the solution that most reliably leads to successful IT implementation is also the hardest one to carry out: changing an organization's information culture.

Nonetheless, preparing the cultural ground is essential. Two professional services companies, which I'll call Company A and Company B, illustrate the impact information culture has on technology implementation. Both companies implemented the same new technology for the same purpose. But while one had an existing information culture that fit the management's objectives for the technology, the other did not.

Company A[4] hadn't had a successful information orientation in the past, and now managers decided it was time to lead with technology. They acquired both a large number of workstations and an organizationwide license for a new software program that combined electronic mail, conferencing, and document distribution. But the company's professionals received little training on how to use the new system. They also had no incentives to share information—only disincentives, especially the fear of giving away their best ideas to others, who would then use them to get promoted in this company's up-or-out culture.

The average professional at Company A worked with few other employees outside his or her office and had little knowledge of anyone else's information requirements. The company recruited new employees based on their willingness to work hard and their training in specific disciplines rather than any demonstrated ability to generate new ideas and package them for use by others. As a result, Company A's fancy new software program was ignored and misunderstood. Even the company's IT sponsor for the program now admits that professionals use the new system mostly for E-mail, a limited application that hasn't solved the main information issues.

Company B, on the other hand, had a long history of hiring people who were good at generating ideas and expressing them in written and verbal form. Managers showed an interest in sharing information long before technology was invented to support this task; the company published regular journals and summaries of press mentions and encouraged its professionals to publish books and articles externally. Company B also had an up-or-out culture, but a key criterion for promotion was whether or not an individual had created and

Valuable tools are still just tools; new technologies alone won't change anyone's behavior.

disseminated new ideas in the form of practice bulletins, articles, or books. Most important, information managers at Company B are just that: in addition to software and hardware, they focus on incentives, organizational structures, human support, and presentation formats as facilitators of good information behavior in the company.

As for information technology, Company B only recently invested in a new system comparable to Company A's. Before that, however, Company B had set up a simple database for key practice and client documents; it had also created a system for measuring the documents that were most commonly accessed, which then counted toward the promotions of individual authors. I never heard anyone at Company B utter the words "information culture"; but by the time an IT platform had been implemented, this company could build on and support a program of information sharing that was already in place. Now its professionals use the expanded software capabilities to facilitate electronic discussions and have created new databases at a rapid clip.

As Company A and Company B reveal, valuable tools are still tools; new technologies, no matter how advanced, won't change anyone's behavior without human intervention. In fact, we have yet to address fully the role of people in information management work, though some research has focused on how information itself affects humans at work.[5] It's not even a matter of "implementing" the right information culture at the right time. The specific solutions to information problems described below demonstrate how information cultures can evolve to match new organizational needs, becoming more human-centered, flexible, and cost-effective in the process.

INFORMATION MAPS

Most large companies now have plenty of databases. But precisely because of the vast amounts of information circulating around organizations, few employees know where to find what they really need. As obvious as it may seem, few companies have an information map that describes the location and availability of the most widely used information. Even at IBM, founder of business systems planning and steeped in the rhetoric of information architecture, executives only recently realized the need for information maps.

Pointers to information in a computer or on a library shelf alone are useful; but pointers to the people who own or oversee particular information are especially valuable. These people can interpret the information, describe its intended uses and limitations, and direct information seekers to other sources. At IBM, a task force studied the use of market-oriented information throughout the entire company. This task force found that market information in regular computerized reports was sometimes ignored by managers—something that other non-IBM research has also suggested. What these managers really wanted was fast answers to their ad hoc questions.

As a result, IBM's task force created the "Guide to Market Information," an internal catalog. The insert "IBM's Catalog of Information" displays a sample page (see page 30). This guide not only lists available marketing information at IBM, but also the people or organizations responsible for that information and how to contact them. It includes proprietary market research, internal and external databases to which IBM has access, electronic bulletin boards, libraries, and internally and externally produced reports. In 1992, IBM printed 5,000 copies, charged internal buyers at cost, and sold out.

Even so, the task force and managers still had to whittle away at old attitudes about information sharing. Some information "owners" were initially reluctant to have their names listed, since they were afraid that answering questions about information would be too time-consuming. In practice, however, the extra time involved hasn't really interfered with anyone's job. Many of these information owners now say they learn from the questions and comments of others. More important, IBM has saved millions by avoiding duplication in the purchase of external market information.

INFORMATION GUIDES

Along with maps, information users need people to guide them to the right kind of information in the first place. Librarians have often performed this role in the past. But while information owners at IBM can answer specific questions, few companies have general guides to the vast information resources available

Hallmark has established "information guides"—translators between information users and the IT staff.

throughout an organization. Once again, including new kinds of human support for technology can help change a company's information culture.

In 1991, Hallmark Cards's MIS managers realized that the company's information users were confused about how to access necessary data. The problem was both technical and behavioral. Financial, customer, supplier, product, and other data were buried in many different databases. In addition, existing applications were hard to use and provided no information about how the data were created.

Hallmark's MIS managers therefore established in each business unit a new full-time position: the "information guide." These individuals are the primary point of contact for anyone at Hallmark seeking computer-based information. They translate between user information requests and the IT staff who can query databases and get the computerized information that users need. Hallmark's information guides have helped improve data access so much that there are now 10 guides around the company. They have substantially reduced the time it takes for employees to find the right information and to compare information across business units.

BUSINESS DOCUMENTS

The form in which information is presented is also critical to its understanding and use. After all, raw data is not information; and accumulating data is not the same as interpreting it and putting it in a usable form. Company B's emphasis on documentation and presentation demonstrates how such an attitude shapes the overall information culture. In that case, promotions and other financial incentives were tied to the kinds of documents professionals produced

In general, business documents provide organization and context, and they exclude enough information so that what remains is digestible. Focusing on which documents an organization needs often leads to a more fruitful discussion than looking at broad information requirements or trying to pin down a term like "customer."

Several companies have begun to identify critical information needs in the form of documents. At Dean Witter, for instance, information managers, particularly those in the central library, were frustrated by their inability to address brokers' information needs efficiently. They advocated hiring more librarians, but financial executives were reluctant to take on additional workers.

With the help of a consultant, finance managers talked to brokers about what information they needed. Instead of phrasing their questions in terms of information and systems, they asked which key documents brokers required. As it turned out, almost all used the same documents over and over. Their needs were categorized into a set of "core documents," most of which were regulatory and reporting documents from U.S. companies.

By separating the documents into three or four industry groups, 90% of the information needed by a typical broker fit on one CD-ROM disk. Dean Witter then created a "perfect information platter," which was updated monthly and kept on a local area network server. By defining common informational needs *and* implementing technology to support what brokers were already doing, Dean Witter was able to reduce its library staff—rather than increasing it as originally suggested— while greatly facilitating information use.

GROUPWARE

Groupware like Lotus Notes, NCR's Cooperation, and Digital Equipment's TeamLinks are excellent examples of less structured information-sharing technologies. This new technology allows teams in different locations to share documents electronically, to discuss issues on-line, and to capture and distribute key information easily.

Even so, companies will fail to take advantage of groupware if they don't also provide adequate training and human support. Indeed, groupware implementation stands or falls on a company's information culture. For one thing, groupware increases the appetite for information rather than controlling it; therefore, companies must provide both the time and training for employees to get used to handling more information. For another, groupware requires people to manage the technology on a regular basis, not just a one-time implementation of the system.

Consider this investment bank, where Lotus Notes has been installed to improve communications and access to external information. The Notes system was linked to several different external databases of information on companies and markets. Individual bankers could specify in general terms the types of information they wanted, and intelligent software (aptly named "Hoover") would then search all these databases and send news items and financial reports on particular companies or deals to the individual desktop automatically. Any banker who later sought information about a topic would also find the results of all previous searches.

Information managers expected this facility would increase information demands and external expenses initially, but demands would taper off since the information could be reused and shared within the organization. They were wrong; demands and costs are still increasing. Yet it also appears that this investment in information now supports the bank's overall business goal: more and better deals. In this case, an unexpected result—increasing information use—led to a clear business benefit that a limited focus on the technology couldn't predict.

In addition, since the database searching and basic communications features of Lotus Notes require little human attention after initial setup—and the system itself is easy to use—the bank's information managers planned a low level of human support. But they didn't anticipate two labor-intensive activities critical to the successful use of groupware. One is training, or more accurately, education: that is, the need to show bankers how the new technology can be used to create better deals and working relationships with colleagues and clients.

Grand IT schemes that don't match what rank-and-file users want simply won't work.

The other important task is the ongoing pruning and restructuring of the system's document databases. Bank managers have found that this task requires judgment and knowledge; if the system made decisions about, say, which documents to delete based on their age, some of the bank's most widely used documents might disappear.

As this use of Lotus Notes shows, even the best new technologies depend on a strong information culture—one that is open, flexible, and expansive. When executives introduce such potentially valuable new technologies, they must be prepared to support an increasing appetite for information. Large appetites may mean further information expenditures. But that's the reality of today's information economy—a reality that can provide better deals, investments, or product planning, as well as new costs, technical requirements, and all-too-human complications.

Some managers have always been distrustful of the information systems approaches of their companies, largely because they didn't understand them. In many cases, they were right to feel uneasy. As the diverse company experiences suggest, grand IT schemes that don't match what rank-and-file users want simply won't work. It certainly doesn't hurt for executives to understand communications networks, complicated databases, and the latest groupware. But precisely because of the enormous financial resources involved, we must abandon the idea that technology in and of itself can solve a company's information problems. No matter how sophisticated an IT system, information is inherently hard to control. It's only when executives stop being "technologically correct"—when they start viewing information as ever expanding and unpredictable—that they realize how little the latest computer application has to do with effective information use.

The Information Facts of Life

1. Most of the information in organizations—and most of the information people really care about—isn't on computers.

2. Managers prefer to get information from people rather than computers; people add value to raw information by interpreting it and adding context.

3. The more complex and detailed an information management approach, the less likely it is to change anyone's behavior.

4. All information doesn't have to be common; an element of flexibility and disorder is desirable.

5. The more a company knows and cares about its core business area, the less likely employees will be to agree on a common definition of it.

6. If information is power and money, people won't share it easily.

7. The willingness of individuals to use a specified information format is directly proportional to how much they have participated in defining it or trust others who did.

8. To make the most of electronic communications, employees must first learn to communicate face-to-face.

9. Since people are important sources and integrators of information, any maps or models of information should include people.

10. There's no such thing as information overload; if information is really useful, our appetite for it is insatiable.

IBM's Catalog of Information

Hands On Network Environment (HONE)

Overview

HONE is an on-line system that provides access to a variety of applications, tools, and information databases designed to increase the productivity of the field. These applications are organized into the following categories:

IBM product information

IBM services information

marketing information and tools

technical information

configurators and tools

financial topics

performance information and tools

administrative information and tools

publications

education topics

customer registration/support tools

about HONE information

Seven components of HONE represent major sources of market information and are described in detail later in this section:

1. Competitive On-Line Marketing Perspective (COMP)

2. EXPERTMENU

3. Market Studies Document Database (MDOC)

4. National Solution Center (NSC)

5. Published Document Database (PDOC)

6. Selected International Account Support (SIASUPP)

7. SERVICES

For further information on any HONE application while using HONE, enter on the command line:

WHATIS application name

Key Contact

HONE Customer Support
External 800-555-6789
Hours 6 a.m.-6 p.m. Mountain Time
Contact the electronic delivery specialist or
HONE coordinator at a local site.

Availability

5 a.m.-1 a.m. Monday-Friday Eastern Time
5 a.m.-3 a.m. Saturday
8 a.m.-1 a.m. Sunday

Responsible Organization

IBM US Services—Electronic Delivery

User Interface/Query

Menu-Driven and/or STAIRS Query Tools

Educational Offerings

For HONE productivity tips and news, subscribe to
HONEINFO Bulletin Board on NATBOARD.
The following educational tools are available on HONE:

- HONE Reference Card—Key HONEREF.

- HONE User Guide—Key GUIDE from the HONE main menu.

- HONEDEMO—On-line demonstrations of selected applications or functions.

- HONE News—On the HONE main menu.

- Application Guides—A number of applications contain User Guides, which may be viewed by keying GUIDE on the application menu.

Notes

1. Albert L. Lederer and Vijay Sethi, "The Implementation of Strategic Systems Planning Methodologies," *MIS Quarterly*, September 1988, pp. 445–461; also Dale L. Goodhue, Laurie J. Kirsch, Judith A. Quillard, Michael D. Wybo,

"Strategic Data Planning: Lessons from the Field," *MIS Quarterly,* March 1992, pp. 11–34.

2. Sharon M. McKinnon and William J. Bruns, *The Information Mosaic* (Boston: Harvard Business School Press, 1992), pp. 162–164.

3. Nitin Nohria and Robert G. Eccles, "Face to Face: Making Network Organizations Work," in *Networks and Organizations,* Nohria and Eccles, eds. (Boston: Harvard Business School Press, 1992). The authors also collaborated on a Harvard case study about Symantec Corporation that illustrates the problem.

4. This company's situation was first described by Wanda J. Orlikowski in "Learning from Notes: Organizational Issues in Groupware Implementation" (Center for Information Systems Research Working Paper, No. 241, MIT Sloan School of Management, May 1992).

5. See Shoshana Zuboff's work on "informating" jobs in *In the Age of the Smart Machine* (New York: Basic Books, 1988).

Originally published in March–April 1994
Reprint 94203

The End of Delegation?

Information Technology and the CEO

PERSPECTIVES FROM THE EDITORS

Executive Summary

INFORMATION TECHNOLOGY NOW PERMEATES EVERY ASPECT OF A BUSINESS, requiring CEOs today to involve themselves in IT planning and decision making. Which IT investment responsibilities should the CEO delegate and to whom? When senior executives consider IT investment options, what should they look for? How do they learn what they need to know to ask the right questions? What role should other managers play in the decision?

Six experts—Bob L. Martin, Gene Batchelder, Jonathan Newcomb, John F. Rockart, Wayne P. Yetter, and Jerome H. Grossman—share their views.

"Information technology risks are becoming increasingly entangled with business risks, and it is therefore the CEO's responsibility to distinguish between them."

BOB L. MARTIN, WAL-MART STORES

"The rules of the IT game have shifted, and [the] function now requires strong general management leadership."

GENE BATCHELDER, GPM GAS CORPORATION

"We do not consider technology investments in isolation. We look at capabilities. . . . If technology is necessary to make a capability work, then [IT] investments are part of the package."

WAYNE P. YETTER, ASTRA MERCK

"I expect my CIO to have a rock-solid business view of technology and my line managers to demonstrate that they understand technology and are using it."

JONATHAN NEWCOMB, SIMON & SCHUSTER

CEOS ROUTINELY FACE QUESTIONS about investment trade-offs. In the case of information technology investments, however, the context for making decisions has changed in the past few years. Once, senior executives could expect their information systems managers to oversee the core processing applications of the business and to help the CEO and line managers make decisions about new IT investments—big ones (American Airlines' SABRE reservation system) and small ones (imaging technology).

Today IT plays a role in most aspects of a company's business, from the development of new products to the support of sales and service, from providing market intelligence to supplying tools for decision analysis. For a global company, the ability to take information from multiple systems and make it broadly accessible to managers and employees is critical. Many observers believe that this fact, along with the increased opportunities for using IT to achieve strategic advantage, requires that CEOs reexamine what they need to know about this resource to manage it effectively.

Which IT investment responsibilities should CEOs delegate and to whom? When they consider IT investment options, what should they look for? How do they learn what they need to know in order to ask the tough questions? What roles should other managers, such as chief information officers and business line executives, play in the decision?

Six experts who have been grappling with these questions share their views.

BOB L. MARTIN *before becoming president and CEO of Wal-Mart Stores' International Division in 1992, was chief information officer of Wal-Mart for ten years. He is based in Bentonville, Arkansas.*

Information technology risks are becoming increasingly entangled with business risks, and it is the CEO's responsibility to distinguish between them. The CEO can no longer afford to delegate these decisions to information systems managers alone. At Wal-Mart and at many other companies, technology has become integrated with almost every aspect of the business. Once, we used technology to run core applications, such as general ledger, or to process key business information, such as sales and inventory. Those were applications that ran on big systems and stood alongside our business. Today technology plays a role in almost everything we do, from every aspect of customer service to customizing our store formats or matching our merchandising strategies to individual markets in order to meet varied customer preferences.

As technology has become pervasive in the business, it has changed the way we work at Wal-Mart. We are placing in the hands of our associates more information than ever in order for them to make decisions closer to the customer and respond quickly to competitive situations. Every company that has, like Wal-Mart, empowered a broader number of employees to make a greater number of decisions knows that this process entails changes in how, when, and where decisions get made as well as challenges in managing the associated risk. I think that CEOs increasingly recognize the impact that technology decisions have on their business and their corporate culture. As a result, they are becoming less comfortable delegating technology decisions to others.

When I'm presented with a proposal to invest in new technology, I look beyond the financial commitment I'm asked to make today and try to understand what my follow-on commitments will be. Technology changes quickly and continually provides capabilities that we may want to take advantage of in our business. We have to know how we will get from the investment we make in today's generation of technology to the next generation.

I also push to understand how well the technology will fit the needs of the people for whom it is intended. As a general rule, a new technology is always a few steps ahead of our ability to use it, and therefore it is critical for executives to manage its impact on those people. If, a decade ago, we had had a greater understanding of the business and organizational dynamics of technology, I think we would now have an even greater payback from our investment in it. In my experience, the new systems that work best are those that are aligned not only with the business but also with the way people think and work.

Finally, we expect any proposed technology investment to reduce the complexity of our business, our processes, or our organization—not to add complexity. I want to see clearly how the capability that the technology supplies will simplify the way we make decisions or the way we accomplish activities and processes, such as moving goods, stocking shelves, or communicating with our suppliers.

For all those reasons, I see fewer investments ahead for us in computing and more—a lot more—in communications. By this I mean that we are shifting our emphasis away from processing systems that give us weekly or biweekly reports (which we have used to manage the business during the following week) and toward technologies that help us move more information out to our associates faster. We're moving away from systems that stand beside our business to technologies that are more integrated with the work of our associates.

Where do CEOs go for help in understanding how technology impacts business today? I find that technology suppliers have become much better at communicating with general managers. In the past, vendors used to send marketers to us. All they wanted to do was sell technology. Today at most of the industry-leading technology companies, the hard-nosed marketers are gone, replaced by engineers and account managers who want to solve business problems for us and are willing to be held accountable for whether or not the solutions deliver as promised. They are more business oriented than their predecessors. Executives can sound them out.

Chief information officers are in a critical role. CIOs who share the language and the vision of the CEO and have a strong link with the business will help the CEO understand the business and organizational risks of new communications technologies.

GENE BATCHELDER *is senior vice president and chief financial officer of GPM Gas Corporation, a Phillips Petroleum Company subsidiary that is located in Houston, Texas.*

My advice to CEOs is this: Your IT function should be run by a great general manager, not by the traditional technology manager. No company can afford to overlook the role information technology can play in spurring organizational change and shaping core business processes. You can no longer delegate the IT function to the back office. Rather, you need to see it as a vital business within your business, run by people with commercial backgrounds who know how to make decisions that are based on ever changing competitive imperatives.

An accountant by education, I have had the opportunity to hold both IT and general management positions during my 25 years in industry. As an MIS manager, I delivered a sizable IT application (an executive information system) and later ran a major corporate data center and worldwide network. More recently, I managed a manufacturing and distribution subsidiary; and now, as CFO of GPM Gas, I'm guiding the reengineering of the corporation's business and commercial processes. These roles have provided me with the unique opportunity to understand the frustrations on both sides of the IT divide. I can see the concerns of IT professionals who must deliver products and services in a strategic vacuum—with a myopic focus on cost reduction—and those of business line managers who question IT's ever escalating costs and seeming inability to focus clearly on critical business needs.

These are old frustrations. It has been six years since I was closely associated with the IT function. But I heard those complaints then, and I hear them now, from managers in my industry and from managers I talk with at other companies. For CEOs to manage information technology effectively in their organizations, they need to address those frustrations head-on—and that means understanding that the rules of the IT game have shifted and that the function now requires strong general management leadership.

Most large companies organized their IT departments to manage an infrastructure built around mainframe computer systems. IT managers and their staffs learned how to run data centers and deliver centralized processing. Today's pace of business requires on-site, on-line information, placing a premium on communications and distributed computing networks. Managers also need this information to be accessible across the business. The new imperative requires companies to integrate systems that have long been isolated from one another; to connect purchasing and manufacturing information with logistics, sales, and customer service; and to connect integrated business systems directly to customers and suppliers. It is difficult, if not impossible, to integrate today's new distributed technologies with the legacy systems that IT organizations have developed and maintained over the years. IT professionals generally don't have the technical and managerial skills necessary to help the company move from these older technologies to new ones.

Worse, they don't have the skills to integrate technology with the business. More and more, business considerations rather than technical ones drive investments in IT. Our businesses are asking, "Why not buy solutions rather than build them?" and "How can IT serve the critical needs of the business rather than those narrowly defined by accounting and human resources?" Far too many IT professionals don't know how to frame questions like these, much less answer them.

I find, in my company and elsewhere today, that it's the general manager who really is leading the changes that new approaches to IT call for. Most line managers are already running full-line businesses these days. Companies transferred bottom-line responsibilities to them in the 1970s and human resource management in the 1980s. They are now ready to take on IT. The CEO needs to help drive this next phase of organizational growth.

We are beginning to move in this direction at GPM. We have established a cross-functional team that is, in a sense, providing general management leadership for our IT function. We refer to this group as our Business Integration Council. It's composed of plant and field operations managers, and accounting and IT staff professionals. The CEO sponsors and fully supports the council. Currently, the group is establishing an approach to systems development that will help us steer our IT in a new direction. We no longer talk about separate systems for accounting, decision support, or technical functions but about integrated business systems.

I believe that teams like ours can help companies solve complex information technology problems. Perhaps they could even manage the entire IT function. Technology and staff managers, working alongside line managers, can solve problems together that require an integrated understanding of both business and technology. The opportunity is there. Today's technology makes it possible. And teams are a tried and true management principle executives have used successfully in many different business situations.

JONATHAN NEWCOMB *is president and CEO of Simon & Schuster, the publishing operation of Viacom in New York City.*

As CEO of Simon & Schuster, I need to understand how information technology is changing our business, and I must ensure that our organization uses technology effectively. Consequently, I spend a lot of my time trying to understand the implications of new technologies, such as the electronic distribution of information products or software programs bundled with books. I also expect my CIO to have a rock-solid business view of technology and my line managers to demonstrate that they understand technology and are using it.

At Simon & Schuster, information technology is not a back-office operation. It is not systems. It is not telecommunications. It is a valuable source of business solutions, touching virtually every aspect of our company. We ship more than 300 million books a year from more than 4 million square feet of warehouses. The books are created from our portfolio of 350,000 active copyrights, each of which has its own complex intellectual property characteristics, such as royalties, rights, and permissions. We simply could not run our business effectively without robust systems to process orders, manage inventories, track royalties and returns, and perform all the other transaction-oriented tasks involved in publishing.

Like many companies today, we use technology to help us streamline business processes, cut costs, and manage independent work activities better. For instance, in creating a publishing product, authors, editors, and layout designers work in parallel with one another. We are installing an electronic manuscript management system that links their activities in a network and that will, among other benefits, help us control these multiple activities better and get products to market faster.

Unlike many other companies, our company is undergoing, because of information technology, a transformation—beyond just the transaction aspects of our business—in the products we create and the core economics of our business. In fact, today more than a fifth of Simon & Schuster's revenues come from technology-based products such as CD-ROMs and interactive television. To succeed in our business for the rest of the decade and beyond, we must be able to package and sell ideas, information, and entertainment in whatever format the customer desires—be it a book, a video, a stream of information and graphics over a computer network, or a combination of all three. We must be able to deliver it to customers when they want it, where they want it, and for a competitive price.

It is for this reason that I need to understand technology and what it is capable of doing. That is not to say that I view myself as a technologist. Rather, I focus on the business needs that the technology supports. I don't need to know about the latest video compression tools. But I want to understand the opportunities video compression may offer Simon & Schuster's Educational Management Group, which delivers live, interactive television to 3,500 classrooms nationwide. What impact might the technology have on the Educational Management Group's operations or on the development of new products? How will electronic manuscript management help us carry content produced for one market cost-effectively into other markets? How will we take, for example, software and curriculum material developed for an educational market into consumer markets? With words and pictures in digital form, can we leverage our creative investments across a greater number of new formats and new markets?

To ensure that I am actively involved in the give-and-take of how technology is used in our businesses, the chief information officer at Simon & Schuster reports directly to me. He has a substantial central staff and has dotted-line relationships with chief technology officers in each of our line units. (The chief technology officers report to their business unit leaders.) The CIO attends the operating reviews for all our businesses and works in partnership with line managers and their technology staffs to design and implement systems that best serve Simon & Schuster's needs and, more important, the needs of our customers. My CIO helps me understand technological advances outside and inside the company and aids me in formulating priorities for technology investments.

I also hold my line managers accountable for technology and make that accountability a part of our regular reporting processes and operating reviews. Line managers must demonstrate a clear understanding of how their own technology programs and products compare with those of their competitors. Technology must figure into their visions for their business: They incorporate technology initiatives into their annual and five-year plans, and those initiatives become part of the management milestones by which they are judged. In other words, technology plays a key role in their strategic thinking, their planning, and, most important, the way they accomplish their goals.

My technology discussions with business unit leaders aren't always formal. I may have an informal discussion with a business unit leader about a product that could have an impact on his or her business. It may be a competitor's product or a product that another Simon & Schuster unit is making. (One of my roles is to help cross-pollinate ideas.) For instance, I might tell the head of my interactive television unit about something our school publishing operation is doing and ask if she sees any way to leverage the technology or the concept in her area.

In fact, we discuss technology actively throughout the company. Chief technology officers meet regularly to trade notes on their operations or to talk about new technology products and ideas. Employees and managers from a number of units and from functions within units come together regularly at informal forums to share information about technology they have explored and to discuss how it might be used in other units. For instance, Simon & Schuster has interactive sites on the World Wide Web. We recently drew together employees from across the company in a one-day forum to brainstorm about ways we could market, sell, promote, and deliver products in this new medium. The point is that we want the majority of our employees to be comfortable talking about technology—and to use it.

New ideas for using technology may originate in the business units and flow up to the company's senior management team or vice versa. In either case, I expect managers to use business criteria to assess technology. The CIO develops multiyear plans with quantifiable objectives for his unit. For instance, he is responsible for setting and reaching rates of return for those systems that are designed to yield cost reductions. Chief technology officers and business leaders also must look at technology investments—whether for systems to help their units be more efficient or for new product initiatives—and treat them as business decisions subject to the same investment thresholds as any other business investment.

JOHN F. ROCKART *is the director of the Center for Information Systems Research at the Massachusetts Institute of Technology's Sloan School of Management in Cambridge, Massachusetts.*

More important than what the CEO *knows* about information technology is how he and key members of the organization *think* about it and about their respective roles in ensuring that the organization uses it effectively. The CEO of 1995 must incorporate the capabilities of IT into his "theory of the business," to use Peter F. Drucker's term ("The Theory of the Business," *Harvard Business Review,* 72 No. 5, 1994). Equally important, the CEO must see to it that key managers envision their roles appropriately.

Organizations fail because their theory of the business is outdated, Drucker argues. As he puts it, the "assumptions on which the organization has been run no longer fit reality." Among the key assumptions are those on "markets, customers, competitors, core competencies, mission, *and technology*" (my emphasis). When the reality underlying the assumptions change, Drucker notes, the organization must incorporate those changes into its theory of the business. In no area are things changing faster today than in information technology. It is a primary job of the CEO to test continually and perhaps change his theory of the business in light of these changes.

In the 1990s, IT has become the fourth major resource available to executives to shape and operate an organization. Companies have managed the other three major resources for years: people, money, and machines. But today IT accounts for more than 50% of the capital-goods dollars spent in the United States. It is time to see IT for what it is: a major resource that—unlike single-purpose machines such as lathes, typewriters, and automobiles—can radically affect the structure of the organization, the way it serves customers, and the way it communicates both internally and externally.

Understanding the importance of the fourth resource and building it into the theory of the business (as well as into strategies and plans) are more important today than ever for the CEO.

First, the capabilities and potential of the technology are increasing more rapidly than ever before. During the past three decades, consumers have received about 30% more computer power each year for the same price. Competition among microprocessor companies and new advances in the technology are accelerating that rate. In communications, the story is similar, if not more striking, as worldwide deregulation, optical fiber, digitization of networks, and the opening up of more of the wireless spectrum are generating even greater increases in cost-effectiveness and capability.

Second, in an increasingly competitive world, IT is critical to the development of more effective operational and management processes. To serve customers well in 1995, companies need to be proficient in a half dozen key areas: reduced cycle times, reduced asset levels (for example, in inventories and people), faster development of new products, improved customer service, increasing empowerment of employees, and increased knowledge sharing and learning. Information technology is a critical resource for accomplishing all those goals.

Third—and perhaps most important with the advent of the "networked age" typified by the Internet, America Online, Prodigy, and the soon-to-debut Microsoft Network—there is now a whole new ball game for ordering and delivering products and services.

The CEO's own vision is the key. It sets a tone. But CEOs cannot do it all. Our ongoing research of IT management suggests that certain key managers determine how effectively IT will be used within the organization. They are line managers who recognize their responsibility for the success or failure of how the IT resource is used and business-oriented chief information officers.

Only line managers are close enough to their business to see the most effective ways to utilize IT. Only they possess the clout to embed IT into their strategies and to commit the necessary financial resources. The CEO's vision can be a catalyst, but it can be multiplied many-fold by line managers who see IT as an essential strategic resource. Thus the CEO, in reviewing strategies and plans, should look for and insist on a relevant and robust IT component.

CEOs also should hold line managers responsible for effective implementation of information technology. Although building good information systems is seldom easy, it is far easier than revolutionizing the process by which people work, their roles, reward systems, accounting systems, or the organizational structure—all of which need to be altered to install today's process-based systems. The heads of IT cannot make such changes. Changes like those are outside of the scope of their responsibility.

The companies that use IT most effectively boast, in addition to good line managers, chief information officers who have a deep understanding of the business and who are therefore capable of building strong working relationships with line management. The CIO's understanding of technology is a given. But it is through a deep knowledge of the business that the CIO can not only understand what is necessary but also build credibility with line managers—and thus build the ability to influence them to move in appropriate technical directions. The CEO's choice of a business-savvy, relationship-building CIO is critical.

WAYNE P. YETTER *a member of the Merck organization since 1977, is president and CEO of Astra Merck in Wayne, Pennsylvania.*

I don't make decisions unilaterally about information technology. On the contrary, I rely on my people and the processes we have in place at Astra Merck to help me understand the opportunities that technology presents and the challenges it can pose. Together, we make decisions about technology investments based on the value of the business capabilities they enable.

To explain what I mean, I must first explain my organization because we are, admittedly, somewhat unusual. In 1992, we began life as a unit of Merck that took to market selected drugs from the pipeline of Astra AB. But the terms of the original licensing agreement between the two companies required that Merck would make us a stand-alone operation (eventually owned jointly by both Merck and Astra) if we reached a specific revenue trigger. By 1993, it was apparent that we soon would reach that revenue level, and we began to plan for life on our own. Astra Merck became a reality in November 1994, when Astra purchased a 50% interest in us from Merck.

Our business is to take products from Astra's
research or those discoveries of other companies that
are licensed to us, guide them through clinical development studies and the U.S. Food and Drug Administration regulatory process, and then market them in the
United States. We had the luxury of building our organization from the ground up. We therefore were able to
think clearly about the processes and capabilities we
needed. So, for instance, we did not organize our business by product lines or functions but by business processes such as licensing, business development, and
management of our unique package of products, services, information, and education for health care professionals, which we call pharmaceutical solutions. We
arranged to have the leaders of each of our process areas
sit on my executive team.

Because we were able to start fresh, we could plan
our information technology strategy at the same time
that we planned our overall strategy, our organizational
structure, our business processes, and our culture. For
instance, we looked at the steps involved in drug development and put into place a process, enabled by technology, that we think will allow us to be faster to market
than our competitors. In our industry, investigators tra-
ditionally have collected data about drug studies at sites
where clinical trials are performed—hospitals and uni-
versities, for instance—and have shipped the information to the drug company. It arrives as an assortment of
separate manually prepared forms, reports, or files. The
company must organize it, manage it, and analyze it,
and eventually incorporate it in documents submitted to
the government. The process has often required keying
information one or more times—and it's prone to error.

We took a new approach. Investigators using personal computers and new pen-based electronic devices collect and ship data electronically from sites directly to Astra Merck on an ongoing basis. We have programmed our computers to confirm with the investigators the accuracy of their entries on the spot. In other words, we wanted to capture the critical information faster and less expensively than competitors. We also wanted to build quality assurance into our collection procedures, not let it be a backstop activity at the end of the process. With these data in digital form, we find that we can store and manage the information more efficiently and can more quickly and easily incorporate it into required documents.

The point is that we do not consider technology investments in isolation. We look at capabilities, such as developing drugs faster or providing customers with services they can shape themselves; and if technology is necessary to make a capability work, then technology investments are part of the package. Starting the business from zero, we didn't have existing processes to reengineer, nor did we have legacy computer systems that are expensive to change and that don't integrate well with new technologies.

Our organization reflects our belief that information technology must be integrated with the business. Our IT people—we refer to them as solution integrators—live and work in the process areas that make up our business. They are not isolated in a support department. They participate in business meetings and help identify ways in which technology can make the business more efficient or more effective. They report both to business managers in the process areas and to the chief information officer. Our CIO is a full member of my executive team, but he is by no means the only technology champion in the group. Every one of my process leaders views technology as a core asset of the business to be leveraged in almost every activity.

To return to my initial point, I don't make IT decisions unilaterally. We were able from the start to put processes into place that would allow the organization to make decisions about initiatives largely by consensus. Every organization has to choose among initiatives. As we began to build Astra Merck, we, too, had to weigh our desires against our resources. First, we had to have the core applications we would need to run the business, such as payroll and telecommunications. We also had to build the capabilities—such as drug development—that would distinguish us from our competitors. We had to decide in what order we would develop our systems and what investments we would make in each.

A program management team made up of managers who reported directly to process-area leaders looked at all the various desired projects and, keeping our resource constraints in mind, established criteria to prioritize them. We expected them to be more than ambassadors from their respective areas and to bring an enterprise-wide perspective to the table. The team also reviewed the interrelatedness of the investments and developed an overall plan for implementing them.

My executive team approved nearly all of the recommendations. The program management team had made most of the really hard decisions about which capabilities to pursue and which trade-offs to accept. They clearly understood our company wide goals and objectives. Their proposed initiatives aligned with our vision and supported our model of the business. Within the executive team, I arbitrated disagreements among my

rs. But in the end we, too, arrived at our deci-
consensus.

As CEO, I ask questions just to assure myself that, in
the broadest sense, the technology under consideration
is appropriate for a given activity. How will the technology differentiate Astra Merck in our ability to serve customers? Can we outsource a specific activity and thereby
avoid the need to invest in it? I also use my executive
team as a sounding board and to ensure that the investment is appropriate and necessary to support our business goals. In the final analysis, I trust my chief information officer, my management staff, and my organization
to use the processes in place to make effective decisions
about information technology.

JEROME H. GROSSMAN *is chairman and CEO of New England Medical Center and a professor of medicine at Tufts
University School of Medicine in Boston, Massachusetts.*

In today's changing health care industry, New England Medical Center must maintain research programs,
teaching facilities, and high clinical-care standards, and
yet also compete on price. New systems and applications
are helping us balance these conflicting demands. It is
my role as CEO to convey the message of change to my
organization.

Historically, hospitals have not competed on price. In
the past, government regulations and insurance reim-
bursement mechanisms created a climate in which we
were paid to dispense service: The more we did, the
more we earned. There was little incentive to manage
costs or quality, and we fragmented our information systems to enable us to track and charge for individual
units of hospital services.

Now, however, in the competitive marketplace of managed health care, the rules of the game are different and the incentives dramatically reversed. Insurers predetermine and prepay for service. At the same time, we still must deliver high-quality service to the patient. Given such imperatives, our information systems must do more than account for provided services. They also must make certain that our quality-assurance systems (for monitoring the quality of patient care) and our cost-control systems provide us with the balanced data we need to manage our conflicting missions more effectively. If we can link together our formerly fragmented systems, we can get an integrated view of patient care that will transform the way we practice medicine, organize and manage care, and relate to each other as providers and patients.

To convey this message at my institution, I have to have answers to the questions that people continually ask: Why change? Where are we headed? How do we get there? What role do I play? Like managers in most companies today, I cannot answer such questions without also talking about the critical role that information technology will play. I work with outside consultants as well as with experts inside NEMC in addressing those questions.

I actively involve several members of my senior management team and other in-house experts in all decisions about IT development and investment. Within the past year, we created the Medical Center Information Services Advisory Committee from top administrators of information services, human resources, quality support services, laboratory, pharmacy, and nursing, plus physician leaders and individuals from a number of clinical services. They are all people who, through their own interests and experience, are knowledgeable about IT applications in clinical settings. The group meets monthly and has a twofold mission. First, the committee defines IT goals and priorities in the context of the strategic plan set by the CEO, the president, and senior hospital managers. Second, the committee reviews and selects IT proposals from our many departments.

The information services department prepares an annual performance report on investments and achievements and compares it with the medical center's strategic business initiatives. We use this report to evaluate the degree to which our information technology infrastructure is helping us become a higher-quality, more effective, and more efficient service provider.

Originally published in September–October 1995
Reprint 95505

IT Outsourcing

Maximize Flexibility and Control

MARY C. LACITY,

LESLIE P. WILLCOCKS, AND

DAVID F. FEENY

Executive Summary

EXECUTIVES PONDERING WHICH PARTS of their information technology function should be outsourced and which should be kept in-house usually ask themselves, Does the particular IT operation provide a strategic advantage or is it a commodity that does not differentiate us from our competitors? If it is a strategic service, they keep it in-house. If it is a commodity—especially one that a supplier claims it can provide inexpensively—they outsource it.

If only the decision were that simple. Between 1991 and 1993, the authors studied 40 U.S. and European companies that had grappled with the issue of outsourcing IT. Their conclusion: The strategic-versus-commodity approach usually led to disappointments.

The underlying assumption of the approach is that managers can place big bets about their markets, future technologies, and suppliers' capabilities and motives with a great deal of certainty. They can't. Even so, many managers sign five- or ten-year contracts without considering that they often cannot predict how business conditions and technologies will change in even two years. They turn to outside providers to gain access to the best technology at a low price without taking into account a provider's need to maximize profits.

Instead, the authors argue, a company's overarching objective should be to maximize flexibility and control so that it can pursue different options as it learns more or as its circumstances change. The way to accomplish that goal is to maximize competition. Managers should not make a onetime decision whether to outsource or not. They should create an environment in which potential suppliers—external as well as internal—are constantly battling to provide IT services.

Executives pondering which parts of their information technology function should be outsourced and which should be kept in-house usually ask themselves, Does the particular IT operation provide a strategic advantage or is it a commodity that does not differentiate us from our competitors? If the operation is a core strategic service, they keep it in-house. If it is a commodity—especially one that a supplier claims to be able to provide for less money than the company's IT department can—they outsource it.

If only the decision were that simple. Between 1991 and 1993, we studied 40 U.S. and European companies that had grappled with the issue of outsourcing IT. Our conclusion: In the great majority of cases, the strategic-versus-commodity approach led to problems and disappointments.

To understand the failure of the approach, consider its underlying assumption: that managers can place big bets about their markets, future technologies, and suppliers' capabilities and motives with a great deal of certainty. They can't. The world is too turbulent, unpredictable, and complex. Even so, many managers sign five- or ten-year contracts without considering that they often cannot predict how business conditions will change in even two years—let alone what technologies will be available. They turn to outside providers to gain access to the best technology and talent at a low price without taking into account how a provider's need to maximize its profits will influence the outcome.

For those reasons, the issue of whether an IT operation is strategic or a commodity is secondary. A company's overarching objective should be to maximize flexibility and control so that it can pursue different options as it learns more or as its circumstances change. The way to maximize both flexibility and control is to maximize competition. To that end, managers should not make a onetime decision whether to outsource or not. Instead, they should create an environment in which potential suppliers—outside companies as well as internal IT departments—are constantly battling to provide IT services.

The explosive growth of the IT industry has enabled companies to create such a competitive environment. In 1989, when Eastman Kodak made its landmark decision to outsource the bulk of its IT operations, there were only a handful of large suppliers from which to choose. Now there are many more. Besides such companies as EDS, Andersen, Computer Sciences Corporation, IBM, and Perot Systems, dozens of niche players now offer specialized services such as mainframe-computer maintenance, applications development, implementation of new technologies, and network management. As a result, organizations have the option of dividing their IT needs into small pieces and awarding them to multiple providers. This approach makes it much less expensive to switch suppliers or to bring a service back in-house if a supplier proves to be disappointing.

The managers of many companies have already embraced such a selective approach to outsourcing. But even they are still feeling their way forward. They realize that the conventional strategic-versus-commodity approach is flawed, but they lack a framework to replace it.

To create such a framework, we studied sourcing decisions in 40 organizations. Most were large corporations, but some were public-sector organizations. We purposely chose companies competing in a wide variety of industries, including airlines, banking, chemicals, electronics, food manufacturing, petroleum, retailing, and utilities. We sought out both successes and failures so that we could identify the practices that differentiated the former from the latter. Approximately one-quarter of the companies had signed long-term (five- to ten-year) multimillion-dollar contracts providing for the management and delivery of all IT services, and about one-quarter continued to have in-house units provide those services. Approximately half the companies we studied had taken a selective approach, outsourcing such services as data-center operations, telecommunications, applications development, and applications support. We conducted nearly 150 interviews with business executives who had initiated outsourcing evaluations (generally chief executive officers, chief financial officers, or controllers), chief information officers, IT staff members involved in evaluating bids and negotiating contracts, outsourcing consultants, and suppliers' account managers.

In the course of our research, we identified some individual best practices for sourcing IT. No one company, however, had combined all of them into a blueprint that others could use. Equally if not more important, none had constructed an analytical framework explaining why such practices worked. What would such a blueprint and such a framework look like? To show how a company's decision-making process could evolve from the conventional approach to the one we advocate, we offer the story of Energen, a fictitious petroleum company based in Houston, Texas, that is a composite of many of the organizations in our study. Energen's senior managers ran up against the limitations of the strategic-versus-commodity approach, came to see that maximizing flexibility and control should drive their sourcing decisions, and then pursued a course that they were able to change along the way.

To Outsource or Not to Outsource

In 1992, the CEO of Energen began to question the company's huge investment in information systems. Over the previous three years, almost every division of Energen had reduced costs by 10% as a result of a major restructuring effort. The glaring exception was IT, whose costs had *risen* by 20%.

To Richard Andrews, the CEO, most of IT seemed like a commodity service. He began to wonder whether the company really needed to own and operate its huge data centers in Houston, Dallas, and New York; its private telecommunications network; and its 2,000 personal computers. When a company he contacted offered to buy Energen's IT assets for $75 million and claimed that it could provide the same service as Energen's IT department for 20% less, Andrews was tempted.

Not surprisingly, Donald Peregrine, the vice president of information systems, tried to change Andrews's mind. He argued that IT was not just an expense: Other departments had been able to cut costs or increase their business because of IT. Andrews conceded that Peregrine had a point and agreed not to make a hasty decision. He assigned John Martin, Energen's CFO and Peregrine's boss, to head a task force to explore the company's outsourcing options.

The task force, which included Peregrine and the vice presidents of the major functional areas, decided to start by dividing Energen's IT operations into two categories: commodity systems and strategic systems. Minimizing costs would be the paramount consideration in deciding whether to outsource the commodities. The commodities that an outside supplier could probably provide as well as and more cheaply than Energen could were the private telecommunications network, the three data centers, support for personal computers, central accounting systems such as payroll, and electronic data interchange.

For the strategic systems, maintaining high levels of service would be the priority. Certain activities were too critical to Energen's business to entrust to an outsider: analyzing seismic data, monitoring quality control in the refineries, and scheduling and tracking oil from the wells, ships, and pipelines. The task force decided to keep those systems in-house for the foreseeable future.

But as the task force members discussed how to proceed, the shortcomings of tackling IT in this fashion became apparent. For instance, they recognized that there were a variety of unknowns—in terms of both technology and issues facing Energen's business—that somehow had to be factored into their decisions.

For example, it was already clear that client-server technology was replacing mainframes and would change the way Energen deployed personal computers. The last thing Energen wanted was to be stuck with outdated technology. So the task force decided that the company should seek only a two-year outsourcing contract for its personal computers.

Another uncertainty was the payroll department. Energen was just beginning to consider whether to outsource the entire department, and Martin, the CFO, thought the company needed to make that decision before it could think about outsourcing the IT system that supported the function. He had not forgotten what had happened several years earlier. Energen had signed a five-year contract with a supplier that would take over a significant piece of the IT system for the company's warehouses even though there was talk about closing some warehouses. Two years into the contract, Energen's management did decide to close the warehouses and had to pay the supplier a large fee to terminate the contract. Not wanting to repeat the same mistake, the task force postponed the decision about outsourcing the payroll department's IT system until the department's future was clear.

Companies should pursue short-term outsourcing contracts whenever they can.

The task force also recognized that although an IT system might be a commodity, it could still be too critical to hand over to an outsider. One example was the telecommunications network that connected Energen's 2,000 gas stations to headquarters. When Energen's managers had first considered outsourcing the network, seven years earlier, they hadn't felt confident that any of the existing suppliers would be able to keep the system up and running. But the problems that had prompted the company to consider outsourcing at that time had not gone away. The infrastructure was costly to manage, and Energen had had trouble retaining top-notch people: Several employees had left for more promising careers at communications companies. In the end, the task force agreed that Energen should see if there were now more qualified suppliers out there.

Just because an IT activity is business-critical doesn't mean that all its elements have to be kept in-house.

The telecommunications discussion sparked a realization: An IT system could be critical but not strategic. That is, a system could be crucially important without differentiating Energen from its competitors. In this light, the task force saw that of the three systems originally labeled strategic, only one—the system for analyzing seismic data—truly was. Although many oil companies that engaged in exploration and production had such systems, the task force thought that Energen's enabled the company to excel in analyzing reserves.

The task force then realized something else: Just because an IT activity was business-critical or even strategic did not mean that all its elements had to be kept in-house. Take the system for scheduling and tracking oil. It was clearly critical and had to be kept in-house, but did the same apply to a major upgrade of the system's software? This question was especially pertinent because Energen wanted to update the software and was going to hire an outside developer for the project. Martin argued that although state-of-the-art software was critical, the software itself would not give Energen a competitive edge, because the company's rivals maintained similar systems. He convinced everyone that Energen would have a better chance of getting the best possible software if the developer was allowed to sell it to other companies.

Choosing Suppliers

Having decided what to outsource, the task force then turned to the job of choosing suppliers. The first step was designing a process. The group concluded that seeking relatively short contracts was a good idea. It also decided that Energen should solicit separate bids for each service. Adopting this approach would ensure that the company could tap suppliers' particular strengths and would prevent any one supplier from ending up with too much power. Peregrine, the vice president of information systems, knew of several organizations that had come to regret their decision to outsource large portions of their IT operations to only one or two suppliers. In one instance, a supplier had charged extra for dozens of services that the company had assumed were covered in the base price and had dragged its feet in introducing new technology.

The members also agreed that they could not automatically assume that a supplier would outperform their own IT department and decided that the department should be allowed to compete when such doubts arose. Peregrine said the data centers were a case in point. The centers had long been forced to satisfy individual users' idiosyncratic needs, resulting in inefficient practices. If his department had the authority to institute best practices, it might be able to operate the centers more cheaply than a supplier, which had to earn a profit. Further, he said, until the department found out how inexpensively the centers could be run, it wouldn't be able to negotiate a good contract with an outside provider.

After the task force agreed on the basic approach to outsourcing, teams consisting mostly of IT managers were formed to request proposals for bids for each contract. With their deep technical knowledge, the managers had the clearest understanding of the company's IT needs. But, fearing that it would be difficult for them to weigh internal and external bids objectively, the task force decided to make the final decisions itself.

The company then started negotiating bids. It found a supplier willing to sign a two-year contract for the personal computers; the deal promised to cut Energen's PC-related costs by 10%. And when Energen negotiated the contract to develop the scheduling and tracking software, it gave the supplier the copyright in exchange for a discount.

The IT department's bid for the data centers was based on a plan for consolidating the three centers into one, thus cutting costs by 30%. That bid was lower than both external bids. One outside bidder then proposed a joint venture with Energen's IT department. Peregrine rejected it. He feared that the combined challenges of consolidating the centers and getting the joint venture on its feet would be overwhelming and that service to Energen would suffer. The department's bid prevailed.

When the task force turned to the telecommunications network, it discovered that there were now qualified providers. Energen awarded a four-year contract for its network to a respected manufacturer of midsize computers that had acquired expertise running its own world-class private telecommunications network. The task force transferred all the employees that had supported Energen's network to the supplier except for two experts, whom it retained to manage the contract.

Because Energen knew what it took to run the network, it was able to hammer out a detailed contract aimed at ensuring that the supplier met Energen's demanding performance requirements. The supplier would have to pay $50,000 the first time network availability fell below 99%, and the penalties would escalate with each subsequent lapse. In addition, if Energen decided not to renew the contract, the supplier would have to cooperate in making the switch to a new supplier. For example, it would have to furnish copies of all programs, data, and technical documentation and also provide installation assistance.

Continuous Learning

The process of outsourcing the personal computers and consolidating the data centers went smoothly. But other transitions were rockier. One lesson that Energen learned was that technical people accustomed to running an internal IT operation could not necessarily make the leap to managing an outsourcing contract.

For example, the two Energen experts retained to manage the telecommunications contract had difficulty understanding that their job had changed. Instead of actually operating and maintaining the network, they were now responsible for interpreting users' needs and communicating them to the supplier. When a technical problem arose, the two experts still wanted to solve it themselves rather than just report it to the supplier's account manager, who argued that technical matters were his domain. Peregrine intervened and recruited one of his data-center managers, who had overseen Energen's hardware leases. The two experts were retained as consultants.

Separately, the company clashed with the telecommunications supplier over the interpretation of the service levels outlined in the contract. For example, Energen had assumed that the 99% availability requirement meant that all nodes on the network had to be up and running 99% of the time. The supplier, however, interpreted it to mean

A company will inevitably clash with IT suppliers over how to interpret the service levels spelled out in their contracts.

that the host node had to function 99% of the time. When links to 20 of its service stations went down, Energen demanded a cash penalty, which the supplier refused to pay.

Six months into the contract, Energen discovered that it could pressure the supplier by offering a carrot. Energen had expanded into the Midwest by buying a regional oil company's service stations in five states. The supplier, which wanted to get the contract for the stations' network, agreed to renegotiate the service requirements. Energen awarded the new contract to another supplier but told the first supplier that if its performance improved substantially, it might win the contract for the new subsidiary in two years, when that contract came up for renewal.

Finally, with the emergence of client-server technology as a cheaper, more flexible alternative to large mainframe operations, Energen eventually decided to outsource the data center. The company was no longer fully utilizing its mainframes, but it didn't want to invest the time and energy to find outside customers for its excess capacity. Another reason to outsource the data center was to free up the company's applications experts to develop programs for the client-server networks. It was unreasonable to expect the programmers both to continue supporting the mainframes and to develop client-server applications.

Did the company regret not outsourcing the center originally? No. As Peregrine had argued at the time, his department had found the most efficient way to run the center, and the company's knowledge of the operation enabled it to negotiate a strong contract later.

The Case for Selective Outsourcing

In confronting whether and how to outsource their IT operations, Energen's senior managers acknowledged what they knew and what they didn't or couldn't know about their business, the course of technology, and the capabilities of outside providers and of the company's own IT department. Then, with the goal of maximizing flexibility and control, the managers sought bids from many suppliers, let the IT department compete for parts of the business, negotiated short-term contracts, postponed some outsourcing decisions, and retained managerial control of business-critical operations. Finally, they realized that deciding to outsource an IT activity isn't the end of the manager's work.

Many managers feel incapable of understanding—let alone managing—IT.

The kind of selective-outsourcing approach we describe in the Energen story may seem like common-sense. But it represents a significant departure from the conventional approach. To managers who take the conventional path, IT is an uncontrollable cost—a function they feel incapable of understanding, let alone managing. And, to make matters worse, they find it a nightmare to attract and retain people who can take care of it for them.

To those managers, entering into a long-term contract with a supplier that purports to have the company's interests at heart—who wants to be a "strategic partner"—seems like the perfect solution. After all, that expert is relieving them of a headache, is often willing to hire their IT people, is enabling them to take assets off their books, and is even willing to pay them for those assets!

The experiences of the 40 companies we studied, however, show that the best alternative to keeping most of IT in-house is not simply to outsource those services. We examined 61 sourcing decisions, which included initial decisions as well as reevaluations and changes in course. Some of the decisions had been made as much as a decade ago. Of the 61 decisions, 14 were to outsource 80% or more of the company's IT budget, 15 were to keep 80% or more of the budget in-house, and 32 were to outsource selectively (operations accounting for 40% of the companies' IT budgets, on average).

Of the 14 decisions to outsource the bulk of IT, senior managers declared 3 out-and-out failures because the expected cost savings never materialized, contracts couldn't be changed when business circumstances changed, and suppliers failed to meet the expected service levels. At the time we concluded our study, 9 others seemed to be at risk of failing for some of the same reasons. Only 2 decisions, which involved outsourcing large data centers—typically the operations easiest to outsource—could be called successful.

Of the 15 decisions to keep most IT services in-house, 5 failed to produce the anticipated cost reductions or service improvements. The other 10 decisions, which led to savings of up to 54%, were successful in the eyes of senior managers, but many users thought that *they* had to pay the price: a drop in service.

Of the 32 selective-outsourcing decisions, 20 met top management's objectives and satisfied most users, too. Only 3 were complete failures. They involved systems-development projects, which are prone to failure whether carried out in-house or by external providers because it's hard to predict how much such projects will cost and how long they will take. At the time we completed our study, it was too soon to determine the outcomes of the remaining 9 decisions.

IT contributes to a company's strategy, and no competent corporate leader would willingly cede control of strategy.

In our view, the disappointing results of the first two approaches stem from some common management failings. Many managers don't fully understand how IT serves individual businesses and operations, the true costs and benefits of IT, and the competitiveness of their

Many managers try to make a system strategic by investing in fancy equipment.

own IT departments. Many companies do not and probably cannot assess the breadth of a supplier's capabilities, especially its ability to cope with new technology. And, finally, the belief that suppliers can be strategic partners is usually wishful thinking. Ultimately, a supplier's need to maximize profits conflicts with a customer's need for good service, low costs, and the ability to change course.

Many managers also fail to see that competitiveness does not come from a single decision: choosing one provider, buying one type of hardware, or investing in one particular piece of customized software. Competitiveness comes from the ability to manage change. If we apply that axiom to IT, it means that companies must have the internal capability to stay on top of suppliers' relative strengths and to scan the horizon for the most useful new technologies. IT, like any major business system, contributes to a company's strategy, and no competent corporate leader would willingly cede control of strategy.

The Sourcing Decision

How should a manager approach IT sourcing decisions? A good way to begin is to answer the following questions:

Is this system truly strategic? We found that most systems that managers consider strategic actually are not. In the companies we studied, only two systems differentiated the companies from their competitors. Managers often make the mistake of assuming that just because a function is strategic, the IT systems supporting that function are strategic, too. Many managers try to make a system strategic by investing in fancy equipment and customized software. All too often, however, they find that even after they spend lots of money, their systems still don't differentiate the company from its rivals, especially given the pace at which rivals can develop similar systems of their own.

Are we certain that our IT requirements won't change? The rise of new technology, of course, will change a company's IT needs. In addition, whenever a company plans to move into a new market or faces potential changes in its existing market, its IT requirements may change. For just that reason, one organization we studied, the United Kingdom's Royal Mail, decided to postpone outsourcing IT until Parliament voted on whether to privatize the postal service.

Even if a system is a commodity, can it be broken off? Many senior executives think of IT as something that can be plugged and unplugged, like an appliance. But most systems are integrated parts of the businesses they support and cannot be so easily separated. Decisions concerning the payroll data center cannot be made independently from those concerning the payroll function. Most IT systems require data from or feed data to other systems and therefore cannot be successfully isolated and handed over to an outside provider. As obvious as it may sound, many managers do not seem to consider that when they make outsourcing decisions. A factory-automation system at one company we studied required data from many functions, including design, inventory control, marketing, and distribution. Because the supplier hired to develop the system did not understand those interfaces, the project took twice as long as predicted and cost twice as much as the budget allowed.

Could the internal IT department provide this system more efficiently than an outside provider could? The assumption behind the strategic-versus-commodity approach is that economies of scale, highly skilled people, and superior practices allow external suppliers to provide IT commodities more efficiently than an internal IT department ever could. We found, however, that many IT departments have equally sophisticated technology and adequate economies of scale but aren't allowed to adopt the best practices that would help them match or beat a supplier's bid. (None of the companies in our study that outsourced the bulk of their IT operations even let their IT departments compete.) Consider the implications: In awarding such contracts to an outside provider, companies are allowing that provider to figure out how to provide the service more efficiently and pocket the savings.

By inviting their IT departments to bid for the contracts, companies accomplish two things. First, they motivate their employees to find ways to provide good service at a lower cost. Of the companies in our study that chose to keep most of their IT services in-house, about half let their IT departments submit bids. Those departments were able to find ways to cut costs by 20% to 54%; not surprisingly, they won the contracts. Second, such companies gain a much deeper understanding of the costs of a given service and the best way to provide it. If they decide to outsource in the future, they will be in a stronger position to evaluate bids and to write a contract that serves their own interests.

Do we have the knowledge to outsource an unfamiliar or emerging technology? A company can't control what it doesn't understand. Many managers think that because no one in the company has enough technical expertise to assess new technologies, they should hand the job over to an outsider. After all, why devote internal resources to acquiring "esoteric" knowledge? Most of the companies in our study that outsourced emerging technologies experienced disastrous results because they lacked the expertise to negotiate sound contracts and evaluate suppliers' performances.

One alternative is to hire a supplier to team up with a company's IT staff on the project. Such an arrangement enables the company to learn enough about the new technology that it can negotiate a contract from a position of strength if it does decide to outsource.

What pitfalls should we be on the lookout for when hammering out the details of a contract?
One of the biggest mistakes companies make is signing suppliers' standard contracts. Such contracts usually contain details that not even a company's legal staff can understand or unravel, especially if the company is outsourcing a technology with which it is not familiar. Among those details might be a lot of hidden costs. In their book *A Business Guide to IT Outsourcing* (Business Intelligence, 1994), Leslie Willcocks and Guy Fitzgerald present the results of a survey they conducted of 76 organizations that had a total of 223 outsourcing contracts. The authors cite hidden costs as the biggest outsourcing problem. The research presented here supports that finding: In virtually every supplier-written contract we studied, we uncovered hidden costs, some adding up to hundreds of thousands—even millions—of dollars.

We also have seen numerous instances in which hidden clauses severely limited companies' options. Managers at one U.S. chemicals company who had signed a contract with an outside supplier for the majority of the company's IT operations tried to lessen the supplier's power by inserting a clause into the contract that would allow the company to solicit bids from other providers if it wanted to develop new software. What the managers overlooked, however, was a clause buried deep in the contract stipulating that the supplier would be awarded the support contracts for any systems developed by other companies—a clause that made the option prohibitively expensive to exercise.

In addition, many suppliers will try to maximize profits by charging exorbitant fees for services that customers assume are included in the contract, such as personal-computer support, rewiring for office moves, or even simple consultations about which equipment to purchase. But even companies that spell out every imaginable detail in a contract have often been frustrated by the unimaginable.

One way for a company to maintain control over a supplier is to withhold a piece of the business contract as a carrot.

How can we design a contract that minimizes our risks and maximizes our control and flexibility?

One way to hedge against uncertainty and change is by creating what we call a *measurable partnership,* in which the company and the supplier have complementary or shared goals. If a supplier is being hired to develop a new application, for example, the contract might stipulate that the company and the supplier will share any profits that come from selling the application.

Another way to maintain control over outsourcing arrangements is to withhold a piece of the business from a supplier and use that potential contract as a carrot, as Energen did with the telecommunications contract for its subsidiary. Or a company can split an IT operation between two suppliers, thus establishing a threat of competition.

A company should also try, whenever possible, to sign short-term contracts. The average total outsourcing contract that we studied was for 8.6 years, but by the third year, most companies complained that the technology provided by their suppliers was already outdated. Short-term contracts are desirable also because they ensure that the prices stipulated will not be out of step with market prices. Consider: A unit of processing power that cost $1 million in 1965 costs less than $30,000 today. Although a supplier's bid to discount IT costs by 20% may sound appealing in year one, the prices in the contract may be well above market prices by year three.

A negotiating team should include the top IT executive and a variety of specialists—but not the CEO.

What in-house staff do we need to negotiate strong contracts? A negotiating team should be headed by the top IT executive and include a variety of specialists—but not the CEO. Many of the worst contracts we saw were broad agreements negotiated by a CEO with the help of corporate lawyers who were equally unschooled in technical details. Although the CEO should not be involved in actual negotiations, he or she must provide the team with a mandate and thus authority with both internal groups and the supplier.

The specialists on the negotiating team should include in-house technical experts with a deep understanding of the company's IT requirements; an IT outsourcing consultant who can translate those internal requirements into the supplier's requirements (former employees of some suppliers now offer such services);

and a contract lawyer specializing in IT who can detect hidden costs and clauses in contracts. In our research, we found that many companies fail to include one or more of those specialists—usually the IT lawyer or the outsourcing expert—on their negotiating teams.

What in-house staff do we need to make sure that we get the most out of our IT contracts? Once a company has decided which services or systems to outsource and has negotiated contracts, it needs another team to serve as contract administrators and service or systems integrators. Some members of this team make sure that suppliers provide the services they are obligated to provide and that all the user's reasonable needs are satisfied. They challenge suppliers when they seem not to be meeting the terms of the contract, deal with disputes over the contract's interpretation, and assess penalties. This team also decides when users are asking too much or too *little* of suppliers. (Many users fail to take advantage of the training that suppliers have agreed to provide.) Such teams often save companies money by making managers think twice before insisting on extraordinary services.

Contract-management teams require people with deep knowledge of the hired providers, the users, and the contracts. Accordingly, they must include individuals with extensive contract-management skills, technical people with a thorough understanding of the company's IT requirements, and a systems integrator to ensure that all IT systems provided by external and in-house suppliers work together without gaps or unnecessary overlaps.

Although it is probably best if the people filling all three roles are company insiders, we have seen many instances in which technical experts accustomed to providing IT services had difficulty adjusting to their new roles as go-betweens. The best systems integrators are typically middle managers from the IT function who have broad knowledge of IT and the organization.

Such a team may need to include as many as 20 people. Few of the companies we studied staffed their teams sufficiently; some had only one person. In addition, many companies underestimated the importance of contract management. Some mistakenly believed that overseeing the contract required little more than assigning someone to review the supplier's monthly bill. And many assigned a technical expert without considering whether that person could manage the complex relationships involved. In contrast, the companies that got the most out of their contracts were usually those that had assigned a manager with experience in administering leasing or licensing arrangements, some IT knowledge, and a proven ability to manage complex relationships.

And the relationships, which span user groups, multiple providers, and the rungs of the corporate hierarchy, certainly are complex. For example, when an employee is added to the computer system, he or she should have to contact only one person—not several suppliers—to have the personal computer and the software installed, to be connected to the local area network, and to be assigned a password for logging on to the mainframe. The contract-management team must guarantee that users receive seamless service.

We also found very few companies with systems integrators. Without such people, users inevitably run into gaps between systems that prevent them from sharing information with other businesses or functions. Fed up with the outsourcing contracts, they start using their discretionary funds to build their own solutions. The result is a hodgepodge—and rising costs, which were what sparked top management to explore outsourcing in the first place.

What in-house staff do we need to enable us to exploit change? To ensure that they always get the most out of IT, companies need a third team of technical experts to help them stay on top of changing technology, changing business needs, and the changing capabilities of available IT providers (both internal providers and suppliers competing in the marketplace). This team can play a significant role in uncovering business opportunities by helping a company understand new ways to use IT. Very few companies have such a group. But without such teams, companies often pay more than they should because suppliers are constantly trying to sell services or technologies that are not included in the basic contract.

One of the team's missions is to look for gaps between the IT the company has and what it needs. With that goal in mind, the team should constantly benchmark the company's IT resources and providers, and should help the company decide whether to change course when an IT contract comes up for renewal.

Another of the team's primary responsibilities is to assess emerging technologies. New technologies such as client-servers, object-oriented systems, and multimedia may sound very tempting, but will the company really be able to take advantage of them? The answer is no or not yet in a surprising number of instances.

Of course, companies can hire consultants to carry out some of this work, but consultants may have their own agendas. For this reason, we think the team should consist of a core of in-house people who can assess suppliers' capabilities and determine which new technologies can best be applied to the company's businesses. Obviously, top management cannot be left out of the loop. All three types of teams must be able to communicate effectively with senior management and command its respect. Without its support, the team negotiating the contracts, for example, cannot hope to overcome the internal resistance from IT personnel and users to changes that threaten their interests or jobs. The team managing the contracts certainly cannot hope to mediate when confrontations between users and providers get out of hand. And the third team has to be privy to top management's thinking about strategy to know what the company will want or need.

The processes that a company uses to manage IT will determine how effectively it controls the IT services it consumes and how quickly it can pursue a different solution when an existing one proves wanting. The companies that excel in developing such processes will end up not merely with superior IT. They will end up with a superior ability to recognize and exploit changes in their markets.

Originally published in May–June 1995
Reprint 95306

The authors would like to thank Rudy Hirschheim and Guy Fitzgerald for their participation in the research that provided the basis for this article. The research was sponsored by the Oxford Institute of Information Management, Business Intelligence (an IT research group), and the University of Houston's Information Systems Research Center.

IT Outsourcing

British Petroleum's Competitive Approach

JOHN CROSS

Executive Summary

IN 1993, BP EXPLORATION OPERATING COMPANY
LIMITED, the $13 billion division of British Petroleum
Company that explores for and produces oil and gas,
outsourced all its information technology operations in
an effort to cut costs, gain more flexible and higher quality IT resources, and refocus the IT department on activities that directly improve the overall business.

BP Exploration took a different path to outsourcing
than most companies have taken. On the one hand,
senior managers decided against receiving all IT needs
from a single supplier because they believed such an
approach could make the IT department vulnerable to
escalating fees and inflexible services. On the other
hand, senior management did not want to divide IT
operations into discrete slices and selectively outsource
all or some of the pieces. The IT department had

experimented with selective outsourcing and discovered that the fragmented contracts required far more management resources than they were worth.

Instead, BP Exploration sought a solution that would allow it both to buy IT services from multiple suppliers and to have the pieces delivered as if they came from a single supplier. To that end, three contractors were hired and required to work together to deliver a single seamless IT service. This arrangement—multiple IT suppliers that act as one—is the cornerstone of the company's outsourcing strategy. The IT department has final accountability for IT services, but it is not mired in the operations. Only by relinquishing operations could IT employees begin to focus on doing business instead of running the business.

In 1993, BP EXPLORATION OPERATING COMPANY, the $13 billion division of British Petroleum Company that explores for and produces oil and gas, outsourced all its information technology operations in an effort to cut costs, gain more flexible and higher-quality IT resources, and focus the IT department on activities that directly improve the overall business. We at BP Exploration, like many other managers at companies across Europe and North America, had concluded that the company no longer needed to own the technologies that provide business information to employees. The market for technology services had matured during the previous decade, and it now offered companies like ours a broad array of high-quality choices. Additionally, the problems encountered in most internal IT departments, with their mix of old and new machines and skills and their traditional tendency to focus on technological details rather than on business issues, distracted senior IT management and frustrated executives. We believed the marketplace offered us an opportunity to trade ownership for results.

Outsourcing was not an end in itself but part of a broader initiative to reshape our IT department. At BP Exploration, information technology was for many years an operations utility: five years ago, we employed 1,400 people to supply processing power to business managers, develop the applications that managers requested, and provide help-desk service and other technology support. Today the operations are gone—delegated to outsourcing providers. We develop few applications ourselves and instead either buy generic applications or contract the work. We reduced our staff to 150 employees; and, over time, they will become increasingly engaged in activities that create real value for the organization, such as working directly with business managers to suggest technologies that will improve business processes, cut costs, or create business opportunities. We want the IT department to help improve business, not to be an internal group whose mission is to respond and supply.

We took a different path to outsourcing than most companies have taken. On the one hand, we decided against receiving all our IT needs from a single supplier as some companies have done, because we believed such an approach could make us vulnerable to escalating fees and inflexible services. On the other hand, we did not want to divide our IT operations into discrete slices and outsource all or some of the pieces. We had experi-

mented with selective outsourcing and discovered that
the disparate contracts required far more management
resources than they were worth.

Instead, we sought a solution that would allow us
both to buy IT services from multiple suppliers and to
have the pieces delivered as if they came from a single
supplier. To that end, we hired three contractors and
required them to work
together to deliver a single seamless service to
our 42 businesses
around the globe. The
short-term agreements
we made with the trio
require them to benchmark their portfolio of services
continually against the IT outsourcing market. We
expect them to subcontract services that can be performed more effectively and less expensively by others
and, more important, to manage those subcontracts.

*The cornerstone of our
outsourcing strategy is a
novel arrangement:
multiple IT suppliers that
act as one.*

This arrangement—multiple IT suppliers that act as
one—is the cornerstone of our outsourcing strategy. The
IT department has final accountability for IT services at
BP Exploration, but we are not mired in the operations.
If we had tried to wear both hats—operations managers
and consultants—we would have failed in our efforts to
transform IT. Most internal IT consultants and senior IT
executives, however much they may try to work directly
with senior managers, inevitably find themselves drawn
back into the day-to-day decisions of running computer
systems. We concluded that only by relinquishing operations could we focus our IT employees on *doing* business, not on *running* the business.

However, we could not allow IT service suppliers to
distract us, either. We could not help improve the busi-

ness if our employees, free from operations, instead became full-time contract managers. We had reason to worry that managing the suppliers would consume far too much of our time. We had experimented with small outsourcing deals for two years before we began to think seriously about how we would outsource most of our IT operations. What we learned is that supplier management can be a headache.

Selective Outsourcing

Beginning in 1989, we contracted selected IT services from a few small and a few large providers. We inherited some of those contracts as a result of our acquisition in the late 1980s of Standard Oil, Britoil, and Lear Petroleum. Britoil's IT department, in particular, had outsourced selected services since 1986. We also signed new, one-year renewable contracts with a host of other providers, including Granada Computer Services for desktop-equipment maintenance in our Aberdeen offices, Hoskyns Group (the U.K. arm of CAP Gemini Sogeti) for help-desk services in our London office, and software companies such as EDS-Scicon for the maintenance and support of select applications used in our North Sea operations. We studied each of these outsourcing deals closely in order to see what they could teach us about the management of relationships, performance metrics, the finances of outsourcing, and control.

We soon discovered that selective outsourcing was an enormous task. To be sure, several of the contracts delivered the benefits we had hoped for: reduced fixed costs, improved service, and access to new ideas and technologies. But the big picture was another matter. Our contracts with suppliers did not provide them with incentives to cooperate with one another. As a result, suppliers managed their own little slices of the pie quite well, but the task of managing intercontract problems fell to us. If a manager in London had difficulty obtaining information from an application running on a machine at our data center in Glasgow, the problem could pass from contractor to contractor: from the help-desk provider in London to a computer systems provider in Glasgow to an applications support provider in Aberdeen to a telecommunications provider to a network support provider, and so on. BP Exploration's IT staff had to take charge of many of these problems and work with all parties to find a solution. We found that we were constantly adjudicating technical issues or solving problems that fell through the cracks.

During this time, we also visited companies outsourcing most, if not all, of their IT operations to a single supplier, and we quickly decided that we did not want to follow their lead. Although a single supplier could provide a seamless package of services and thereby free us from managing the pieces, such an arrangement posed other problems we wished to avoid. When a company cedes control of IT to a single provider, it becomes dependent on the quality of the supplier's skills, management, technology, and service know-how. In today's dynamic IT services market, no one company can excel in all these areas. Linking its destiny to a single supplier prevents a company from taking advantage of the many innovative, high-quality technologies and services offered by others in the market. Worse, a supplier's capabilities may wane over the life of a contract as its competitors' wax.

We looked for an alternative that would combine the flexibility and control of selective outsourcing with the comprehensive service offered by a single provider. We knew that we did not want to lock ourselves into long-term contracts with our outsourcing partners. A couple of the companies we visited had signed ten-year contracts with their suppliers, essentially freezing the companies into technology solutions that were no longer meeting the needs of their changing businesses. Their suppliers could provide new solutions—for a price. Instead, limited-term contracts would better allow us to change technology solutions to match our business needs. And yet the suppliers would have to make a profit from the deal, too (which they usually do in the later years of a long contract and through fees for extracontractual services). How could we make all that happen?

First, we had to put our own house in order. To improve service and reduce the cost of duplicated systems incurred through our acquisitions, in 1989 we consolidated seven IT departments into a single global IT department with centralized financial control. We then proceeded to standardize systems across the company. For instance, Houston used one system to simulate oil reservoirs, Alaska another. In fact, we had eight different simulation systems operating within the company. We reduced the number to two and eliminated the staff supporting the other six systems. Similarly, we reduced the number of drilling, geology and geophysics, and other systems.

Over the next two years, as we experimented with selective outsourcing, we closed all but two data centers. By consolidating systems and data centers, we reduced the size of our staff by half—and cut our costs by more than 25%. Through these and other measures (such as consolidating maintenance contracts), we made our operations as efficient as possible before handing them over to service companies. It seemed imprudent to allow suppliers to reap millions of dollars in profits from changes we could make ourselves. We wanted them to earn their pay by pushing the performance of our operations beyond the performance we were capable of.

Finally, we created an atmosphere of understanding throughout the organization. BP Exploration's senior managers instilled the belief that the company should focus on a minimum number of core processes. They encouraged managers throughout the company to debate the merits of outsourcing activities that were not core to professional service companies. Rather than support a large IT staff year after year, for instance, why not hire outside contractors only as they are needed for a

Rather than preselect a list of providers, we seriously considered any provider of information-technology services.

given project? In other words, why not turn fixed costs into variable ones wherever possible? As business managers became intrigued by the opportunities offered by the "disposable environment" for outside noncore services, they set a supportive tone within the organization that made our efforts possible.

Then we turned our attention to the market. Rather than preselect a list of providers, we decided to immerse ourselves in the IT services market. We seriously considered any interested provider. Because we were certain that we would hire more than one contractor, we did not need to limit our search to companies that could provide a full array of IT services. We could—and did— consider data-center management companies, applications development groups, telecommunications companies, and organizations that did some or all of those things. In November and December of 1991, we mailed

100 Request for Information packets to large and small providers in the United States and Europe, including each of the providers servicing our existing short-term outsourcing contracts, every major provider in the market, three internal management buyout bidders, and a number of companies we had never heard of—several of them military services companies hunting for commercial contracts.

The Request for Information outlined our intention to refocus our IT department and summarized the scope of the work we intended to outsource. The body of the document contained more than 30 questions intended to help us get a sense of a particular provider's experience and approach to outsourcing, its geographical reach, technical capabilities, and policies for managing costs and improving efficiency. Our questions also probed for information about cultures, business strategies, human resource policies, service philosophies, and quality initiatives. From the responses to these questions, we hoped to learn about how service companies operated, how they made decisions, and how flexible they were—in other words, we hoped to get a sense of the range of our options. More specifically, we asked companies to elaborate both on their experiences as lead suppliers or as subcontractors to other suppliers and on any service provision partnerships they may have had with other suppliers.

Sixty-five companies responded to our inquiries, providing us with a wealth of information about the market for IT services—in particular, the strengths and weaknesses of all major and most minor players. To assess the responses thoroughly, a team from the IT department, along with specialists from BP Exploration's internal audit, contracts, materials, and commercial departments, met off-site in February 1992. Rather than have all 20 people study all 65 responses, we assigned each person 3 or 4 responses and asked him or her to champion the companies in presentations and discussions. This exercise forced our people to concentrate on the strengths and weaknesses of the companies and to consider each as a serious candidate.

Through these discussions, we whittled the list down to 16 companies. During the next few months, senior IT managers visited all the companies. We looked closely at each company's management staff and culture, the depth of its understanding about the outsourcing industry, and its strategic vision. Several of the companies we visited did not have a clear vision of their market. The senior managers—even the board of directors—were not entirely sure of the markets they were targeting or of how they saw their markets evolving. Those companies did not inspire our confidence.

We also tried to assess the company's ability to be innovative and flexible. In particular, we looked for indications that a company was entrepreneurial, service oriented, and aggressive about keeping overhead costs down. Although we were candid with the suppliers about our IT costs and probed to see how receptive they might be to novel fee arrangements down the road, we did not talk about the estimated cost of providing services to us. In fact, we did not discuss costs with potential suppliers until the final stage of the interviewing process. We concentrated first on trying to make our outsourcing vision for IT work and then on trying to make it work at the right price.

BP Exploration's top-level executives agreed with this logic. A board of executives, chaired by John Bramley, BP Exploration's chief financial officer, closely reviewed the progress of our search for service providers. In fact, the board, encouraged by the capabilities of several of the companies we interviewed, expanded the scope of our original outsourcing agenda to include the IT services for BP Company's offices in London and Harlow. The board also advised us to negotiate an incremental approach to outsourcing with prospective providers. In keeping with the decentralized culture of British Petroleum, the board asked us to seek the buy-in of each of the businesses to the outsourcing initiative; as a result, we could not guarantee to suppliers that we would turn over to them the worldwide scope of our operations in one fell swoop. As it turned out, we outsourced major sites in the United Kingdom before extending the practice to the United States and other, smaller overseas sites in the following months.

Assessing the Short-list

After our interviews with the 16 U.S. and European companies, we pared the list down to 6. We had initially planned at this stage to give our short-list of suppliers a detailed description of our specifications and to ask for proposals. But now, with our list developed, we wondered if there was a better way to proceed. After all, what we needed was a way to assess how suppliers on the short-list would work with one another. We had begun to doubt that we could strictly enforce seamless service from more than one provider through contracts. If we picked three vendors and insisted that they work together as a team, we might find that their cultures did

Suppliers met around the clock—testing capabilities, forming alliances, dissolving them, and forming new ones.

not mesh. Inevitably, disagreements would arise among them, and we did not want their disagreements to disrupt service to us, nor did we want them to look to us for adjudication. Was there, we asked, some way to enlist the companies in the search for the answer to this question? It would be better for us if the companies themselves could develop a plan to provide seamless service and take responsibility for making it work.

We devised an innovative way to do just that. Having secured their agreement in advance, we gathered with all six suppliers for a weeklong interactive workshop. The ground rules that we set were simple: We wanted an alliance of suppliers to formulate a proposal to meet our specifications. The alliance had to be composed of more than one supplier and fewer than five. We would set challenging cost-performance targets. And the six suppliers would develop proposals in close collaboration with one another.

As we hoped, suppliers met round the clock to explore what each could do—testing capabilities, forming alliances, dissolving them, and forming new ones. At the end of the week, the six companies submitted five different proposals representing an array of alliances. Most important, they had devised solutions for our needs among themselves and took responsibility for providing those services.

The proposal we eventually accepted, submitted by Sema Group, Science Applications International Corporation (SAIC), and Syncordia (a subsidiary of British Telecommunications that last year became part of Concert, a joint venture of BT and MCI), met all our expectations. Unlike other proposals, these three companies could show how they genuinely complemented one another. Sema Group excelled in managing traditional data centers and commercial engineering applications. SAIC, a military systems company based in San Diego, California, could implement modern distributed computer systems and develop leading-edge technologies and scientific applications that could enhance our upstream oil business. Syncordia had the experience, reach, and flexibility to manage our complex telecommunications services.

Sema Group, Syncordia, and SAIC were able to provide the mix of generic and customized IT services that we required.

Sema Group agreed to run our United Kingdom data center in Glasgow (now moved to Sema's own premises in Birmingham and Glasgow), to run the BP head office computer center in Harlow (now consolidated into another Sema facility), and to provide IT services for BP Exploration's offices at Stockley Park and British Petroleum Company's head office in London. SAIC would manage the IT facilities for BP Exploration's European headquarters in Aberdeen and all the company's applications support except for those applications running at our Alaskan facilities. Syncordia would manage our telecommunications and telex networks, providing data, voice, and video communications throughout the United Kingdom and to most overseas sites except Alaska. (At the time, our Alaskan unit was exploring outsourcing arrangements of its own.)

Although European "antitrust" laws prevented the three suppliers from joining in a formal alliance to deliver services to us (we have a separate agreement with each company), the companies agreed to provide combined services to all our sites. They also agreed to accommodate the variety and diversity of our needs. For instance, all our offices worldwide need telecommunication services, networks of personal computers, access to corporate financial databases, and help with any computing problems that may arise. But our production facilities in the North Sea and Alaska require help-desk services 24 hours a day, seven days a week, whereas our London offices need help-desk services only during work hours, Monday through Friday. Sema Group, Syncordia, and SAIC could provide this mix of generic and customized services.

The trio also agreed to a plan to provide the seamless service that was so important to us. For each of our eight major business sites—London, Aberdeen, Houston, Anchorage, Bogotá, Stavanger, Stockley Park, and Sunbury-on-Thames—one of the three suppliers serves as the primary contractor and coordinates the services the trio provides to most or all of the businesses supported by the site. For instance, SAIC took responsibility for IT in Aberdeen and for businesses and operations reporting to Aberdeen, such as the Sullom Voe oil terminal in Shetland. If a manager in Shetland has trouble with a system, responsibility for the problem isn't passed from supplier to supplier. SAIC must make the system work for the manager. The cause of the problem may not lie in SAIC's own systems; it may be the result of a glitch in the telecommunication slinks managed by Syncordia, in the data center managed by Sema Group, or in the complex interactions of all three companies. To solve the problem, SAIC's technicians and managers must work closely with employees of the other two companies, but SAIC alone is ultimately responsible for making the system work again. To the manager in Shetland, it appears as if SAIC is the single provider of a seamless service.

BP Exploration business managers at each of the eight major sites negotiate with our IT suppliers for customized services. The similar framework agreements between each provider and BP Exploration define the generic services provided, the legal provisions, the general commercial principles of financial targets, margins and incentives, quality assurance, performance reviews, and a host of other issues across the company. Working within these framework agreements, each site negotiates its own contracts, specifying the scope of services, service levels, and performance targets. At some sites, the BP management team negotiates only with the primary provider for delivery of all services. But seamless service does not mean seamless negotiations at every site. Because of the complexity of the services involved, managers at our largest site, Aberdeen, must deal not just with SAIC but with all three providers. Ultimately, the business units pay for the IT services they receive. Suppliers directly invoice the sites, and the sites recover costs from their business units.

We scrutinize those costs closely. The three suppliers' books are open to us; they itemize all costs clearly in quarterly or annual invoices, distinguishing among direct, allocated, and corporate overhead costs charged to BP Exploration. Additionally, Syncordia manages all our telephone charges with third-party operators and provides us with comprehensive records. Our agreement stipulates that we can audit our suppliers' accounts of services to us, if it is necessary.

Each year, we negotiate new performance contracts with our suppliers. Initially, many of the measures we used were familiar ones in IT, such as response time, mean time between failures, and time to fix. We are about to begin using a balanced scorecard to set measures for the value we derive from services. With the balanced scorecard, suppliers will receive points for innovation, business process improvement, financial management, customer focus, and organizational learning. The sum of the points will determine the margin that suppliers earn on the direct costs of delivering service to us. We can weight the scorecard to suit prevailing business conditions at each site. The specific metrics for the scorecard and several of the other details are still under negotiation and will not be introduced until June 1995.

From time to time, we benchmark our suppliers against services of comparative quality and scope provided by other suppliers in the market. The framework agreements require our suppliers to deliver the best in a given area. If we believe that another provider can supply a more cost-effective or strategically important service, we can insist that the relevant provider subcontract the work and manage it. This arrangement, as vexing as it is to our suppliers (it was one of the most difficult provisions to negotiate), should allow us to take advantage of fast-paced changes in the marketplace.

We have not yet had to require a supplier to subcontract work, but one did voluntarily. When Syncordia took over responsibility for our telephone service in Scotland, it immediately terminated a contract we had with BT, Syncordia's parent, and assigned the work to another company that was effectively servicing a number of our other locations. Syncordia determined that the second company could do the work more cost-effectively, in turn allowing Syncordia to meet its own cost commitments to us more effectively.

Our suppliers win, too. They receive an agreed-on remuneration for the year. Additionally, if a supplier can reduce the operating costs for a given service below the targets we set for it, it can keep 50% of the savings. Therefore, while the total revenue from a particular service diminishes to BP Exploration's benefit, the effective margin on that revenue increases to the supplier's benefit. And there are other benefits. Because of the reputation all three companies have earned working for us, SAIC increased its commercial business with other companies outside the United States, Sema landed contracts in South Africa and the Far East, and Syncordia won additional business with other British Petroleum companies.

Finally, we kept the length of our outsourcing contracts short. We did not sign ten-year contracts with our suppliers, as so many other companies have done with IT service organizations. In February 1993, we signed five-year framework agreements with Sema Group and SAIC, and a two-year contract with Syncordia, which we renewed this year—but not without seriously considering a competitor's bid. The market for telecommunications is extraordinarily volatile, and we believe prices for most telecommunications services will fall dramatically in the next few years even as performance rises. We will want to revisit our decisions about telecommunications continuously to make certain we are getting the best value we can. The market for IT services isn't quite that fast-paced, but ten years is an era in IT, and contracts of this length could potentially lock us into services that become outdated before the contract expires.

Confronting Challenges

Our outsourcing strategy has not always worked smoothly; we have encountered some bumps. Indeed, the first few months of the implementation were rocky.

While senior managers at BP and at the three suppliers clearly understood the vision of seamless service captured in the framework agreements, their respective operations staffs did not. One supplier's employees looked to us to set directions for them, as they would in any traditional outsourcing contract. They wanted to follow orders, whereas we insisted that they look for ways to make the operations run more efficiently and effectively. Another supplier staffed a site primarily with former BP employees (who under the agreement became employees of the supplier) and very few of its own managers. As a result, the services we had long supplied to ourselves continued as if nothing had changed; the supplier did not bring in any new ideas or improve the operations. Eventually, the suppliers replaced middle management at the sites, and the situation improved quickly.

Our suppliers are not only allies but also rivals competing for our business. Therefore, they can be reluctant to share information.

Some of the blame for those early challenges rested with us. We mistakenly set cost reduction as the most important target for our suppliers to achieve during the first year. The provider that added too few of its own staff to our former IT site, for example, was working under particularly stringent cost targets. In 1994, we shifted the emphasis from costs to service responsiveness, quality, and customer satisfaction.

Today we are not yet entirely free from the task of managing conflicts among our suppliers. They work well together to deliver day-to-day service to us, in part because they are so interdependent. (Because they are each lead contractors at some sites and subcontractors at others, they are careful to help one another meet their commitments to us.) But they are also rivals competing for our future business. As a result, they are reluctant to share, for instance, best practices with one another. If a company responsible for one site, say, solves a common problem with the interconnections between different personal computers or develops a help service that BP business managers at the site like, that company is reluctant to share this information with its two competitors. Why? Because the knowledge or service may become part of the supplier's pitch for additional business during future contract negotiations. We are currently exploring ways to encourage our suppliers to share this kind of information more readily.

Managing change among our competing suppliers is also challenging. For instance, we are upgrading our telecommunications network, in essence redefining the way data will flow from company to company around the globe. To accomplish this, we must have a set of common protocols. But for competing suppliers, protocols are a battlefield. BP's adoption of one standard over another may affect the balance of either company's future business with us. If we did effectively choose one company over another, we would contradict our efforts to outsource our operations to multiple suppliers. We want our suppliers to compete and to cooperate. To that end, BP Exploration employees are working with them to find a solution agreeable to all parties.

On the whole, the relationships between BP Exploration and the providers are good. As their service managers become more fully engaged in BP Exploration's internal management processes, the suppliers gain a greater understanding of our requirements. At many sites, supplier employees work side by side with our staff, helping to deploy technology to support business-process reengineering efforts or to find new ways to make our systems more flexible and less expensive. BP employees worked with staff from all three providers to upgrade local area networks at our Aberdeen site. Supplier employees brought technical knowledge to the project (and SAIC employees managed it), while BP employees provided an understanding of the business needs the project had to meet. In addition, supplier employees often participate in our staff meetings and make suggestions (not always IT-related) to improve the business.

Both sides have gained a greater understanding of the other's expectations. Our negotiations with our suppliers have become easier since then. Our initial negotiations in 1993 over performance goals took two months. In 1994, we set performance targets in a week. And we concluded negotiations over our 1995 performance contracts in just one afternoon. Business customers report that they can see a vast improvement in service.

We continue to expand our outsourcing activities. In 1994, we signed similar IT framework agreements with two additional IT service companies. We outsourced our applications support for Alaska jointly with Alyeska Pipeline Services Company (which manages the Alaskan pipeline and is jointly owned by BP, Arco, Exxon, and other companies) to Computer Task Group (CTG). I-Net manages the data center and IT services in Houston. CTG and I-Net must work closely with the other three suppliers to provide service to us—the seamless service that we have come to expect. For instance, SAIC provides all computer services with the exception of applications development in Alaska, and CTG must work closely with them. BP employees in Alaska expect CTG to solve any problems that might arise—not to shrug the problem off as another supplier's responsibility. Similarly, I-Net and SAIC have teamed up to provide services for us in Bogotá, Colombia.

Our IT costs continue to fall. Through consolidation and outsourcing, we reduced our IT staff by 80%, and our overall IT operating costs have fallen from $360 million in 1989 to $132 million in 1994. We have increased the proportion of IT costs that are variable and adjustable to business conditions. We have gained greater flexibility in our systems and higher quality IT services. And it has become increasingly apparent that service companies provide us with technical skills and ideas that we could no longer develop inside our own company. For instance, we are exploring ways to use virtual-reality technologies, such as desktop teleconferencing and other multimedia applications that facilitate virtual meetings, to enhance organizational effectiveness inside BP. The most innovative technologists in this field want to work for small leading-edge companies, not big oil companies. While we could offer premium salaries to lure top-drawer virtual-reality specialists, in the end we would pay more for the technology trying to create a virtual-reality group within the company's walls than we would buying services and applications directly from the market.

Most important, we are actively repositioning IT to be the service group we envisioned in 1989. In fact, in our efforts to focus on IT issues that directly aid the business, our 150 remaining IT employees are fast becoming internal consultants. We are only beginning to understand how to do this effectively: How should we organize our emerging consulting group? How do we work effectively to help senior managers identify technology solutions? What are the pressing business issues we need to address? For instance, we increasingly believe that we can play an important role within BP Exploration by helping the organization manage business information better. Currently, when we drill a well, we collect a vast amount of technical information and can make this available to project teams drilling elsewhere. But we don't systematically collect information about how the political relationships were managed, how agreements with other companies were negotiated, or how environmental issues were addressed. Because we don't collect the knowledge that we gain from business experiences such as these, the organization as a whole rarely benefits from it. We're looking at techniques to bundle and manage this information systematically.

More immediately, BP Exploration eliminated regional operating companies in 1995 so that our 42 businesses—major exploration ventures, production sites, pipelines, and so on—report directly to our global management group in London. We need to understand how to manage our consulting group's resources to help the businesses communicate effectively.

To meet these challenges, we may look outside BP Exploration once again—this time to the external consulting market. We are considering a number of new avenues. For instance, we have discussed forming a partnership with an external consulting firm, which would help us draw new talent and new ideas into our IT department, including consultants who have worked extensively with senior business managers. At the same time, such a partnership might allow our employees to get outside the walls of BP to work on projects in other companies, thereby broadening their experience and improving their consulting skills.

We have also discussed the possibility of outsourcing part of our IT consulting practice to another firm or to our suppliers. It is an idea, an option. Our experience with outsourcing has convinced us that today's market for so many different kinds of business services allows us the luxury to consider options none of us thought possible a few years ago. Ultimately, whatever decision we make will be aimed—as it has been from the beginning of our efforts to transform the role of IT within BP Exploration—at focusing our internal energy as effectively as possible on the work we are in business to do: profit from finding and producing hydrocarbons.

Originally published in May–June 1995
Reprint 95302

How Continental Bank Outsourced Its "Crown Jewels"

RICHARD L. HUBER

Executive Summary

NO INDUSTRY RELIES MORE ON INFORMATION than banking does, yet Continental, one of America's largest banks, outsources its information technology. Why? Because that's the best way to service the customers that form the core of the bank's business, says vice chairman Dick Huber.

In the late 1970s and early 1980s, Continental participated heavily with Penn Square Bank in energy investments. When falling energy prices burst Penn Square's bubble in 1982, Continental was stuck with more than $1 billion in bad loans. Eight years later when Dick Huber came on board, Continental was working hard to restore its once solid reputation. Executives had made many tough decisions already, altering the bank's focus from retail to business banking and laying off thousands of employees. Yet management still needed to cut costs and improve services to stay afloat. Regulators, investors, and analysts were watching every step.

Continental executives, eager to focus on the bank's core mission of serving business customers, decided to outsource one after another in-house service—from cafeteria services to information technology. While conventional wisdom holds that banks must retain complete internal control of IT, Continental bucked this argument when it entered into a ten-year, multimillion-dollar contract with Integrated Systems Solutions Corporation. Continental is already reaping benefits from outsourcing IT. Most important, Continental staffers today focus on their true core competencies: intimate knowledge of customers' needs and relationships with customers.

T HE CONTINENTAL BANK I JOINED IN 1990 was an institution in the final stages of a crisis. In the late 1970s and early 1980s, Continental had participated with Penn Square in large-scale energy-related investments. When falling energy prices burst Penn Square's bubble, Continental was stuck with more than $1 billion in bad loans. That disaster led in 1984 to a run on Continental by institutional funders and a liquidity crisis, requiring an FDIC bailout. By the time I came on board, Continental executives had made many tough decisions. Thousands of employees had been let go, and the bank had fundamentally altered its business focus—moving out of

Eyebrows rose, heads shook, and tongues wagged when Continental decided to outsource IT.

retail banking and becoming an all-business bank. Yet these changes had failed to ensure Continental's continued survival. There was still work to do.

One obvious place to start was to search for ways to cut costs in order to devote relatively limited resources to the bank's strength: establishing and maintaining secure business-customer relationships. The search ended in Continental's now celebrated passion for "outsourcing"—hiring vendors to do the work of many of the bank's in-house service departments. Our decision to outsource management of the bank's employee cafeteria and other peripheral services, including even legal services, caused little stir in the banking community. However, our decision to outsource almost all of our information technology—the first money-center bank to do so—was something of a revolution. Eyebrows rose, heads shook, and tongues wagged when Continental, in December 1991, signed a ten-year, multimillion-dollar contract to buy information technology services from an IBM subsidiary.

It was one thing, banking analysts and competitors said, for an institution to spin off a portion of its technical operations, as First Fidelity Bancorp had done in 1990. But why would Continental decide to surrender nearly complete control over IT? Was management intent on cutting costs because the bank was in worse financial shape than people had suspected, or was it hoping to make Continental an attractive acquisition target?

Neither. Continental did not give up control over its information technology strategy. Nor was it positioning itself for a sale or desperately seeking to raise cash. The bank outsourced its information technology when senior managers became convinced that outsourcing offered the best way to service the customer relationships that form the foundation of the bank's business. For me, the decision sprang almost naturally from Continental's banking philosophy and the premium it places on serving the customer. Persuading other bank employees, many of whom feared losing their jobs and some who feared for the bank, was more difficult. But, as I believed almost from the start, it was the correct decision, and our experience in the first year since we began outsourcing has confirmed my initial instincts.

Starting Over

Eight years after Penn Square, Continental's hangover still lingered. In response to the crisis, Continental had been overhauled. The teller windows in the lobby were gone, signaling the end of Continental's aspirations to serve retail banking customers. Our energies were now focused on business customers and wealthy individuals, the type of clientele that demanded increasingly personalized banking services.

We still had a way to go to restore the bank's financial footing and its once rock-solid reputation. Frankly, Continental's reputation was weak in 1990. Our profits were still under pressure. Regulators, investors, and bank analysts watched the bank's every move. Successes usually evoked only faint praise. Missteps—and there were some—were cited as proof Continental would never fully recover from its near collapse.

Regulators, investors, and bank analysts watched every move. Successes evoked only faint praise. Missteps were cited as proof Continental would never recover.

Chairman Tom Theobald, who had joined the bank in 1987, had split Continental's business in two: originating loans and packaging and selling them to investors. Our goal was to become a complete financial intermediary, arranger as well as principal in transactions, employing the bank's balance sheet as a warehouse in which assets would be stored until they could be sold to outside investors. To succeed, we needed strong links between the two arms of the business. That called for teamwork across functional lines that quickly mobilized bankwide resources to satisfy customers' needs.

We're good bankers—not specialists in running cafeterias or legal services.

What we didn't need was any function that distracted the team from its main job as financial intermediary. In order to get a clearer picture of what might be available for outsourcing, management in the second quarter of 1990 undertook a product evaluation process in which it divided the bank's activities into three categories. The first group included profitable activities critical to the bank's core clients: small, midsize, and large businesses (nearly half of which are privately held) and wealthy individuals. This is Continental's traditional franchise; these activities were not touched. The second group included overseas investments made to ease Continental's debt exposure in South America. While these were unrelated to our clients' needs, they were nevertheless profitable and, therefore, were not touched. The third group, anything that didn't fall into the first two, quickly became "endangered species" or prime candidates for outsourcing.

By year's end, the bank had spun off food, security, messenger, property management, and legal services.

While we considered ourselves nimble bankers, we had no special expertise in other areas that make up a large organization—operating cafeterias, for example, or running a law firm. Perhaps half of Continental's problems with in-house services stemmed from overuse. For instance, the most routine documents were always sent to the legal department for review. "Better safe than sorry," people would say, while thinking, "and besides, it's just an internal cost, not real dollars." Since Continental has outsourced legal services, we've become a more demanding consumer, and we've reduced our legal fees considerably.

That happened time and again: after turning to outsiders, the bank saved money and received better service. Within our corporate culture, outsourcing began to gain momentum. So it was not surprising that many outsourcing proposals were floating around the bank in late 1990, among them one for information technology.

By early 1991, I was responsible for the bank's back-office and data-processing operations. These areas were a source of great frustration. Everything the information technology unit did took too long and cost too much. The more I learned about the situation, the clearer it became that the bank was already effectively outsourcing technology services to a group of people who happened to work at the same company I did but whose work was different.

Four problems stood out:

First, and most important, the bank's existing mossback mainframes couldn't respond quickly and flexibly to customers' needs. Once the pride of the IT operation, these old machines simply could not perform in a market where product life-cycles are measured in weeks.

Second, in trying to end-run the inflexible mainframe problem, a Balkanized mess of small desktop systems and databases had proliferated that suited only the needs of individual business units. To solve this problem, the bank's IT staff sought to develop an integrated IT architecture that would respond to customer needs and adapt to flexible business processes. The goal was to provide consistent information across the corporation and permit the rapid delivery of market-driven products—all while minimizing the cost. The in-house staff made progress in 1990 and 1991, and work on it continues today at Continental's outsourcing vendor.

Third, like most other large organizations, Continental had chronic staff headaches. The bank used to employ about 500 people in the IT unit, about half the number needed for major systems upgrades or large conversion projects and about twice the number needed for day-to-day maintenance. Moreover, top technical people didn't want to work at a bank, where IT assignments paled in comparison with the opportunities at companies that focused on technology.

Finally, money was a problem: staying on top of breaking technology required huge investments. As I turned these problems over in my mind, I was far from certain we could resolve them by ourselves. Eventually, I came to believe it was probably not in the bank's interests even to try.

Defending the Crown Jewels

When outsourcing IT was raised at Continental, I was already fairly immune to technology's charms. My experience in the banking business had taught me that information was a tool clever bankers used to their customers' advantage, but managing it was not a banker's core competency, as some of my banking colleagues seemed to believe. In fact, it often appeared that the more a bank thought it knew how to manage technology, the more likely it would end up being manhandled.

I was a group executive at Citibank in June of 1986 when it purchased Quotron. That was a real eye-opener. I watched my colleagues, so confident of their ability to comprehend and manage information technology, spend hundreds of millions of dollars to buy the market-data-distribution company and hundreds of millions more trying to make it work. Citibank, of course, was not alone. Many banks, including Continental, invested heavily in technology over the years, but so far, no bank's technology has led to a truly dominant position or locked other players out of the market. Today I attribute Citibank's failure partially to its misguided belief that banking is first and foremost an information business.

While there is no doubt that manipulating data is important in any bank, conventional wisdom holds that banks must retain complete and secure internal control of IT. Surrendering control would endanger a core competency—or so the argument goes. In my view, however, two elements of the banking business far outweigh the importance of information technology: intimate knowledge of customers' needs and relationships with customers. At Continental, these are our core competencies, not the ability to run an IT department.

Citibank's mistake was looking at banking as first and foremost an information business.

Continental aims to spend its time and money furthering its central strategy, which can be summed up in a single sentence: serving as a financial intermediary between client needs and the markets. We provide tailor-made products to satisfy an individual customer's requirements and strive to provide new, integrated services to help clients manage their money and their risks. The raw materials that make up these products are information and technology, commodities that change almost every day. And access to them is what is important. What is not important is owning the computers, employing the technical staffers, and managing the operation.

What's important is access to information, not owning the technology.

As I pondered outsourcing at Continental, I wondered, what makes us think that a group of bankers can manage technology as efficiently as technically advanced people can? Doesn't it make sense to devise a banking strategy and then hire the best technological talent to create, provide, and maintain the software and hardware needed to support the strategy? Doesn't it make sense for a Formula One racer to drive the car instead of build it?

Skeptics—inside the bank and then outside the bank after word spread that Continental was considering outsourcing IT—asked, "What about proprietary technology? Isn't it the equivalent of a bank's crown jewels?" My answer is "No." Years ago, proprietary technology could produce large profits, but these days, proprietary technologies, for example, cash-management products that can take years and huge investments to produce, are cloned in months or even weeks.

Competitive advantages from information technology no longer accrue naturally to institutions that have internal technological "resources." Rather, the benefits accrue to institutions with the flexibility to tap the source of the best technology at an acceptable price. Look at the steel industry. For years, U.S. steelmakers argued that the Japanese could never mount a significant challenge to their domination of the American market. But their argument was flawed—they believed the Japanese would never be a factor in the steel business because they lacked local access to coal, iron ore, and other necessary natural resources. Today Japan produces the highest quality steel in the world—precisely because local supplies are unavailable. The reason: steelmakers are free to buy materials wherever the price/quality ratio is most favorable.

The implication for banking is clear, and by March of 1991, most Continental senior managers favored outsourcing IT. While there was no detailed plan, a growing consensus held that if the bankers could concentrate on what they do best, using the best technology available, customers would benefit. Managers believed outsourcing would give the bank better access to the cutting-edge technologies we wanted; cut the development time for new, technology-driven products; and transform the bank's IT costs from fixed to variable.

The last factor, while important, was not the chief priority. Meeting customer demand was number one. Costs for outsourced IT when business was running at highest capacity could exceed expenditures for in-house IT. But, presumably, periods of high capacity would generate high bank profits, which would underwrite the higher costs. The benefits of outsourcing would come into play during the inevitable periods when demand slackened and the bank could easily reduce IT expenditures. With senior colleagues largely convinced, all I had to do was persuade the rest of the company. Then I had to find Continental's perfect technology partner.

Reality Testing

Preparing a group of people for what will likely be a major change requires a delicate touch. The bank wanted the input and acquiescence of both groups of employees affected by outsourcing: the bankers and traders who used the technology and the technical staffers who would either end up working for another company or need to look for another job. We did not want to rush ahead without considering employee concerns; nevertheless, I wanted to spur the process onward.

The first thing we did, in March 1991, was establish a formal process to study in detail the feasibility of outsourcing IT. Because senior management was leaning heavily toward the general concept of outsourcing, the study was aimed less at analyzing outsourcing risks and more at overcoming them.

We hired a consulting firm that was experienced in outsourcing to measure internal sentiment and identify potential land mines. The consultants' "reality testing" among 100 key business and IT managers generated surprisingly little resistance to the idea, probably because of the success Continental had already had outsourcing so many other bank functions.

However, seeing the consultants' presence as evidence their jobs were at risk, IT employees worried a lot. As their anxiety mounted, productivity fell. Looking back, I am sure their uneasiness was compounded by the lack of a detailed outsourcing plan. That was our first slipup in the process. If we had defined our intentions better, employees might have been more positive. As part of our communications plan, we were having regular discussion sessions between IT workers and senior managers about outsourcing proposals and their potential impact on employees. IT workers were responding well, but if I had to do it over, I would keep things under tighter wraps until we had a detailed plan to present to employees.

The next step was the visible and well-communicated establishment in May of the organizational structure to guide the bank through the outsourcing decision. We formed two councils to evaluate options. The business council, which I chaired, was made up of managers from the bank's most important businesses and was responsible for strategic and business recommendations to the board of directors. The technical council, which did most of the real work, conducted detailed analyses to evaluate and select vendors.

Members of the technical council were the top technical people drawn from all the bank's businesses: the private bank, corporate bank, trading floor, and cash management. Unlike senior managers, they were by and large doubting Thomases. But a handful of factors nudged them toward management's position. First, management had decided that even if we outsourced IT, we would retain a cadre of technically literate businesspeople on staff to manage the relationship between the bank and the IT vendor. Second, the choice of the technical council chairman was critical. I chose a technical person from one of the business units with a great deal of credibility among his banking peers, rather than the chief

My corporate mantra: disaggregate, disaggregate, disaggregate.

information officer or someone else from the IT unit. I thought the person I chose would bring more of an open mind and a greater sense of urgency to the process.

Third, the formation of the council itself helped move the process in the right direction. Members had to look beyond their discrete areas of expertise to the broader horizon of the entire bank's IT needs. As their meetings continued, council members began to recognize, as I had earlier, that pursuing in-house solutions was, in fact, outsourcing technology to an internal shop. Gradually, the possibility of a strategic partnership with a reliable outside company began to take hold.

Fourth, the technical council members received detailed instructions about what their job was and how to do it. Their charge was to make a recommendation. They could urge the bank to outsource some IT functions and retain others, but a simple vote against outsourcing IT was not acceptable. To reach their recommendation, they were asked to break down IT into its separate elements and examine the risks and advantages outsourcing posed for each. That made the evaluation process less threatening, which proved once again the merit of what has become my corporate mantra—disaggregate, disaggregate, disaggregate.

The technical council's work advanced quickly—it had just two months to report—and discussions soon boiled down to the two most sensitive areas: maintenance of existing systems' software and development of new applications. One-third of the members believed Continental had to control maintenance of the banking applications that it bought from outside vendors. For this faction, the key was not the application itself but its maintenance after it had been customized. Another third, the council members with the strongest business biases, dismissed concerns about maintenance but insisted the bank keep development of new applications in-house. The final third thought we should outsource everything.

The council tackled the maintenance of existing software first. Those who wanted to retain control over maintenance put up a fierce fight. But the team broke down the tasks involved and evaluated the work each employee performed. After that, most objections started falling away, and achieving consensus on outsourcing the development of new applications was comparatively easy.

An additional factor that helped smooth the way for outsourcing was the bank's early consideration of regulatory issues. In the wake of the S&L scandals, in which outsourcing deals were employed to inflate artificially the net worth of some banks, regulators have focused closely on accounting treatment, asset valuations, fees, and service levels in banks. We attended to these issues from the outset and consulted frequently with regulators as the outsourcing decision progressed.

Choosing Partners

With the backing of the technical council, we had gained consensus from bank managers and staff. Now could we hire the best company available to take over IT? Rather than react to what vendors were offering, management first reexamined the bank's strategic objectives and listed the benefits outsourcing would provide:

- Technology improvements, particularly an improved ability to put advanced technologies to use without bearing the huge costs of network integration and applications development.

- Strategic enhancements, including more time and resources to focus the organization's attention and long-term investments on its fundamental business-banking franchise; improved business-unit involvement in and control over software; better use of internal resources; and an enhanced ability to manage IT when user demand was shifting and investment spending was uncertain.

- Financial gains achieved from drastically cutting the IT payroll, converting technology costs from fixed to variable, and leasing the bank's data center and selling its equipment.

- Improved management and better IT budgeting.

By outsourcing its IT in the summer of 1991, Continental beat other banks and took advantage of a competitive shakeup in the technology business. Management also made a decision that, in retrospect, was critical. It opted to retain legal and financial consultants, specialists in large outsourcing transactions, to assist in structuring and conducting the bidding, as well as the evaluation, selection, and contracting processes.

The request for proposals called for the vendor to assume responsibility for most of the functions and services that Continental's in-house IT staff was performing: processing, network engineering, development of new applications, and maintenance of new and existing software. Specifically, the vendor would:

- Purchase all existing equipment and network hardware.

- Assume financial, administrative, and legal responsibility of the hardware and software Continental leased.

• Provide use of our data center to other outsourcing customers and pay Continental for that use.

• Employ all bank employees who performed the functions the vendor was assuming in comparable positions with comparable pay and benefits.

Two of these points merit amplification. First, the sale of equipment was a smaller part of the financial arrangement than people might imagine. For some banks, the sale of up-to-date equipment (of which Continental had quite a lot) could lower their capital/asset ratio, but that was not the case at Continental. The bank had already written off most of its older equipment. The hardware sale was a small gain for Continental, a footnote to the larger transaction.

Regarding the bank's IT workers, the concern was both practical and altruistic. For the most part, these people were loyal employees who deserved the bank's concern. Despite the fact that there had been much to fault in their department's performance, the bank needed their protection during the vulnerable transition period when word was filtering out that Continental was thinking of outsourcing and also after the deal was closed. By pledging to defend their interests, the bank kept these people on board.

Moreover, the bank needed to ensure that several of its longtime technical employees joined the outsourcing vendor because they were the only people who knew how Continental's systems actually worked. Like most systems that have developed over time, Continental's was not well documented. Until it is or the system is replaced, the employees who carry the documentation in their heads are a critical resource.

The bank's "employee protection plan" failed to cover one employee, however, and caused the most awkward and painful incident of the whole outsourcing process. I didn't see that the bank's chief information officer, a talented and valued employee who had helped resolve some of the bank's IT problems and who was at the center of the outsourcing debate, would face a painful conflict of interest as potential vendors approached him to try to win support for their proposals. This was understandable, but it was also unacceptable. My solution, which admittedly was not elegant, was to offer him a choice: either sign a binding agreement vowing to reject job offers from vendors involved in the bidding (the offers or the hints of them had begun to surface) or accept a strict consulting arrangement with the bank that would exclude him from the bidding and evaluation process but permit him to talk to any potential vendor. He reluctantly accepted a consulting position and later joined a partner of the vendor we selected as a consultant but with no role in our outsourcing deal.

The request for proposals was issued to three companies after lengthy talks with consultants, potential outside vendors, and others: Andersen Consulting, Computer Sciences Corporation, and Integrated Systems Solutions Corporation, IBM's outsourcing subsidiary. As the scope of our proposal became clear, ISSC decided to take on a partner, Ernst & Young, to handle the sensitive area of applications development if ISSC's bid was accepted.

We evaluated responses against several criteria, three in particular: the vendors' ability to address the bank's specific technological needs, their plans for the bank's IT staff, and pricing for a ten-year contract. Pricing was complicated. So complicated, in fact, that we brought in yet another consultant to guide the three evaluation teams through the thickets of various pricing offers and ensure that they did not compare technological apples and oranges.

My colleagues and I assumed the bidding process would go through two rounds, and it did. While Andersen submitted competitive proposals, ISSC's was the most attractive from the start. That was a mild surprise, given IBM's reputation as a competent but slow-moving giant. ISSC handled our case nimbly and generously. Its proposal included sweeteners that cost ISSC little but were valuable to Continental. For example, ISSC offered more than 1,000 IBM personal computers and software as part of the package. The bank also felt comfortable with Ernst & Young, with whom Continental had had an extensive and productive relationship. In an attempt to wring every advantage out of the bidders, the bank instituted a second round, a 30-day negotiating period with ISSC and another vendor. They each gave their last, best shot, and in September, Continental accepted the ISSC proposal.

Contract talks followed—three long months of intense negotiations that represented the most active and demanding phase of the outsourcing project for all participants. The bank was determined to gain much tighter management control over information technology by outsourcing. That required designing new, stricter methods to measure and document progress, then incorporating them into contract terms and pricing.

To appreciate the complexities of this process, consider trying to figure out how a successful project should be billed from start to finish. How do you pay for projects that are changed in midstream or cancelled? How do you ensure the bank receives full value from the technology alliance? The solution we arrived at was based on function-point analysis, a new method of precisely measuring work in terms of the "business functionality" delivered to the bank. Unlike past contracting practices that relied on a vendor's best estimate of the person-hours a job would require, function-point analysis breaks every project into functional units. It thus gives the bank and ISSC a firmer grip on the nature of the work to be performed and its cost.

Other issues were then hammered out—issues like data confidentiality and security, termination rights and responsibilities, inflation adjustments, volume measures and pricing, transition costs, and cancellation penalties. Finally, on January 1, 1992, Continental switched from building information technology to buying it.

Reaping Rewards

After one year, the relationship with ISSC has been tested and is working well. We were prepared for transition problems regarding machines and employees. More than 400 former Continental IT employees had to learn to treat people they used to work with as clients and adapt to a new culture at ISSC. In fact, the personnel transition is probably the project's most striking success story. Continental employees are treated as valued customers by their former coworkers. I credit this to the cooperative management structure we established at the outset. Continental remains in complete control of its basic technology strategy. The bank sets strategic directions and establishes project priorities, content, and budget. It counts on ISSC for technological resources and methodologies and

Business units companywide now work together to make IT decisions.

Ernst & Young for development support to provide the tools Continental bankers need. ISSC and Ernst & Young clearly understand their roles in the relationship.

Inside Continental, we also understand our roles and priorities. A technical oversight group (TOG), made up of representatives from the bank's business units, balances the technological requirements of individual units with the bank as a whole and decides which projects we will contract out and which must wait. Individual fiefdoms used to stake out priorities. Now they must submit IT proposals to the TOG for evaluation, which ranks them on a bankwide scale of priorities. Our business units are working together as a result, sharing expertise and information to ensure that technology costs are allocated appropriately across the company.

Another key component of the new arrangement is a 20-person team, the cadre of technically literate employees management pledged to form. These highly knowledgeable businesspeople understand IT and the services the bank is buying. Thanks to this group, which advises bank units on technology projects, communication between ISSC and Continental has been open and effective. The head of the bank's corporate technology group meets with the ISSC project head every Friday morning to review projects and resolve problems. Some members of this group also spend time looking over the horizon to the next technological breakthrough and plotting a path to it.

Continental is also fortunate that ISSC has offices nearby in the bank's former data center. The bank retained a skeleton crew for maintenance and backup on-site, but routine maintenance and troubleshooting, such as responding to last year's Chicago flood, is the responsibility of ISSC employees. They travel only about ten blocks from their offices to Continental headquarters. The bank's former employees now working for ISSC have greatly widened their career opportunities by switching from what was essentially a glorified mailroom (important but not central to the bank's business) to a real technology company. Continental also has access to a larger pool of technical talent; ISSC hires more help when necessary.

We estimate that the arrangement with ISSC will save Continental $10 million a year, but because no one can foresee what technologies will be required in the future, no one can predict the long-term savings accurately.

At the technical level, the bank is making progress toward its overall and business-unit technology plans. Both the bankwide integration of information technology (the plan Continental adopted in 1990 but could not follow through on) and development of new computer-driven applications are proceeding on schedule, with strict controls in place. New applications for the trading floor are coming in quickly. And a survey of technology's impact on private banking, the kind of project that would have taken Continental's old IT operation months to complete, was delivered in two weeks.

Through painful experience, Continental Bank is aware that it is easy to develop an IT system whose surface elegance disguises internal chaos; that's a pretty accurate description of the bank's worst experiences with in-house IT. Now the administrative controls the bank needs are in place at every stage, from the dollars it spends with ISSC through data security and disaster recovery.

Another obvious success is the changed behavior of the bank's business units. They are now active and disciplined participants in the IT process. With virtually all

IT work on a hard-dollar, contract basis, they are devoting time on the front end of projects to define clearly and carefully their technology needs and how they want to spend their budgets. In the old system, they used to wander down to the computer shop and kick an idea around with the guys. The process is more demanding today, but it's paying off in reduced technology costs and improved quality. In short, the IT outsourcing agreement has given Continental, at a reasonable cost, the technological arsenal suited to the next generation of banking.

Creating a Technology Alliance

MY EXPERIENCE RIDING HERD over Continental's decision to outsource IT taught me five important lessons about transforming a technology alliance from an attractive concept to a manageable transaction.

1. **Focus on business, not technical decisions.** Technology issues can easily confuse the basic question of whether outsourcing is feasible at a realistic cost. Once that question is answered in the affirmative—at Continental, it was answered quickly and intuitively—questions of how the partnership is to be set up follow as negotiating and contract issues.

2. **Keep a lid on.** Open, honest, credible communication is important, but to preserve staff morale and productivity, it pays to keep preliminary testing, feasibility studies, and vendor screening quiet until a plan for outsourcing is relatively advanced. Some Continental employees were needlessly distressed when they heard management was

considering some undefined idea to outsource IT. While we did a good job of corrective communication, we should have given the employees who were not directly involved in the decision a clearly defined plan that incorporated the realistic assessment of prospects, decision points and schedules, and the range of options for employees.

3. **Decide early how you will manage the relationship with your outsourcer.** Define the organization and roles for the partnership early in the process, not after the agreement has already been reached.

4. **Create ways to ensure technology integration and "ownership" at the business-unit level.** Managers must understand that once IT is outsourced, internal buffers will no longer insulate them from technology decisions. These decisions will be their responsibility, like any other business decision.

5. **Don't go it alone.** Outsourcing IT means more than selecting a vendor. Organizations need considerable analysis and help, frequently from experienced consultants, to be sure they choose the right partner and negotiate an agreement that will work well over the long term.

Originally published in January–February 1993
Reprint 93102

Managing by Wire

STEPHAN H. HAECKEL AND
RICHARD L. NOLAN

Executive Summary

RATHER THAN FOLLOW THE MAKE-AND-SELL STRATE-
GIES of industrial-age giants, today's successful companies focus on sensing and responding to rapidly changing customer needs. Information technology has driven
much of this dramatic shift by vastly reducing the constraints imposed by time and space in acquiring, interpreting, and acting on information. In order to survive in
this sense-and-respond world, big companies need to
consider a strategy that Stephan Haeckel and Richard
Nolan call *managing by wire*.

In aviation, *flying by wire* means using computer
systems to augment a pilot's ability to assimilate and
react to rapidly changing environmental information.
When pilots fly by wire, they're flying informational representations of airplanes. In a similar way, managing by

wire is the capacity to run a business by managing its informational representation.

Rather than investing in isolated IT *systems,* a company must invest in the IT *capabilities* that it will need to manage by wire. Indeed, coherent corporate behavior needs more than blockbuster applications and network connections; it must be governed by a coherent information model that codifies a corporation's intent and "how we do things around here." More important, a coherent model must include "how we change how we do things around here."

Companies like Mrs. Fields Cookies, Brooklyn Union Gas, and a financial services organization that the authors call Global Insurance are managing by wire to varying degrees, from "hardwiring" automated processes at Mrs. Fields to a complete enterprise model that codifies business strategy at Global Insurance.

F LEXIBILITY AND RESPONSIVENESS NOW RULE THE MARKETPLACE. Rather than follow the make-and-sell strategy of industrial-age giants, today's successful companies focus on sensing and responding to rapidly changing customer needs. Information technology has driven much of this dramatic shift by vastly reducing the constraints imposed by time and space in acquiring, interpreting, and acting on information.

Responding to the competitive dynamic created by information technology, many large companies have drastically downsized, divested, and outsourced to reduce the costs and complexity of their operations. Yet simply reducing the size of a corporation is not the solution. As CEO Jack Welch has said, GE's goal is not to become smaller but to "get that small-company soul and small-company speed inside our big-company body." We believe that corporate size is worth saving. Market power, not bureaucratic clumsiness, can again become the dominant quality of a large corporation. But in order to survive in a sense-and-respond world, big companies must consider a strategy that we call *managing by wire*.

In aviation, *flying by wire* is a response to the changes introduced by jet-engine technology in the 1950s. It means using computer systems to augment a pilot's ability to assimilate and react to rapidly changing environmental information. Today heads-up displays (computer-generated pictures projected onto the pilot's helmet visor) present selected abstractions of a few crucial environmental factors, like oncoming aircraft and targets. Instrumentation and communication technologies aid in evaluating alternative responses. And when the pilot makes a decision, say to take evasive action by banking sharply to the left, it's the computer system that intercepts the pilot's command and translates it into the thousands of detailed orders that orchestrate the plane's behavior in real time.

When pilots fly by wire, they're flying informational representations of airplanes. In a similar way, managing by wire is the capacity to run a business by managing its informational representation. Manage-by-wire capability augments, instead of automating, a manager's function. Fly-by-wire technology—and by extension managing by wire—integrate pilot and plane into a single coherent system. The role and accountabilities of the pilot become an essential part of the design. Autopilot, or complete automation, is used only in calm, stable flying conditions.

The system design allows for considerable flexibility in pilot behavior, including the ability to override the technology if, for instance, a sudden storm arises.

Like a plane at mach speeds, a company must be able to respond to threats in real time. In today's turbulent business environment, strategies have to be implemented in tactical timeframes. In response to this challenge, top-level managers need to view information technology in a new light. Rather than investing in isolated IT *systems*—such as e-mail, reservation systems, or inventory control systems—a company must invest in the IT *capabilities* that it will need to manage by wire.

The ideal manage-by-wire implementation uses an enterprise model to represent the operations of an entire business. Based on this model, expert systems, databases, software objects, and other technical components are integrated to do the equivalent of flying by wire. The executive crew then pilots the organization, using controls in the information cockpit of the business. Managers respond to the readouts appearing on the console, modifying the business plan based on changes in external conditions, monitoring the performance of delegated responsibilities, and sending directions to subsidiary units such as manufacturing and sales.

Of course, if the enterprise model represents the wrong reality—or is incomplete, out of date, or operating on bad data—the outcome could be catastrophic, like putting engines in reverse at 30,000 feet. Creating a robust model of a large business organization is an extremely challenging undertaking. But companies like Mrs. Fields Cookies, Brooklyn Union Gas, and a financial services organization that we will call Global Insurance have already demonstrated the feasibility of representing large portions of businesses in software. These companies manage by wire to varying degrees, from "hardwiring" automated processes at Mrs. Fields Cookies to a complete enterprise model that codifies business strategy at Global Insurance.

Many companies have spent decades automating pieces of their businesses, scattering networks and incompatible computer platforms throughout their organizations. But the empowered, decentralized teams of the information economy need a unified view of what's happening within an organization. Coherent behavior requires more than blockbuster applications and network connections; it must be governed by an enterprise model that codifies the corporation's intent and "how we do things around here." More important, a coherent model should include "how we *change* how we do things around here." Adding the institutional ability to adapt in a dynamic environment has become a survival imperative for most companies. And this ability will ultimately differentiate a manage-by-wire strategy from the static make-and-sell strategies of the past.

Hardwiring a Business

Over the last three decades, companies have used information technologies in increasingly sophisticated ways to run parts of a business. From the mainframe complexes of the 1960s to the client-server platforms of today, computers already help executives manage by automating business processes, from payroll to cash-dispensing. In fact, a company like Mrs. Fields can build an extensive representation of its business by automating procedures, that is, by codifying them in software.

In small companies, the model of "how we do things around here" often resides in the minds of a few people. Under these conditions, if senior executives are willing to sacrifice some flexibility and delegate the technical design to IT professionals, it's possible to represent enough of the business in software to manage by wire.

Mrs. Fields uses software to issue advice to local managers, such as how many batches of cookies to bake.

For example, Mrs. Fields Cookies has captured a significant amount of its well-defined business in software. Its hardwired processes resemble the autopilot capability of a fly-by-wire system.

In 1978, when Debbi Fields opened her second cookie store in San Francisco (45 miles away from her first store in Palo Alto), she confronted the logistical problems of maintaining hands-on management at remote locations. She and her husband Randy, a skilled computer professional, had ambitious expansion plans that would prevent Debbi from personally overseeing each store. They needed a strategy that would let them know what was going on in hundreds of dispersed locations and at the same time ensure that local managers responded to daily challenges in the same way Debbi Fields would. In this case, Randy Fields had the technical expertise to implement in software the way Debbi Fields worked. He created the software at a reasonable cost and much more quickly than most traditional large-company IT groups could have.

Now with more than 800 stores, including franchises around the world, the central management of Mrs. Fields uses software to issue instructions and advice to store managers. Each morning, local managers project sales for the day and enter information into a personal computer: for example, day of the week, season, and local weather conditions. The software analyzes this data and responds with hourly instructions on what to do to meet the day's objectives: how many batches of different cookies to mix and bake; how to adjust the mixtures as the actual pattern of customer buying unfolds; when to offer free samples; how to schedule workers; and when to reorder chocolate chips.

There are a few fundamental principles that define Mrs. Fields's business concept: a thorough articulation of "how we do things around here"; a conviction that quality must be centrally controlled; and a dedication to knowledge sharing between central management and local store managers. As a matter of policy, the company integrates all of its information in one database and has one set of guidelines about how things are done the Mrs. Fields way. Because this vision is so clearly articulated, and because the company's business niche is relatively well-defined and stable, top management has, in effect, created an informational representation of Debbi Fields in each store.

Yet a manage-by-wire system that hardwires much of a business can turn out to be too rigid. For example, because its software was designed to describe the behavior of U.S. store managers, Mrs. Fields faced a number of challenges when it expanded into Europe and Asia, where different labor laws, languages, and supplier contracts had to be taken into account. In addition to the adjustments required to accommodate a wider range of local environments, falling profit margins forced the company to become more flexible in the way it applied information technology to running its daily business at remote locations.

Responding to these new conditions, Mrs. Fields Software (a separate business unit) developed a second generation of software, called the Retail Operations Intelligence system. ROI contained modules for inventory control, scheduling daily activities, interviewing and hiring, repair and maintenance, financial reporting, lease management, and e-mail. Senior management believes that ROI can be adapted to a variety of retail and service organizations. In fact, Mrs. Fields sold ROI to Burger King in 1992.

But at Mrs. Fields, top management relies on its IT division to translate business strategy into software. If senior executives want to change how the business runs, IT professionals must change the procedural software code. Because the cookie business doesn't change significantly from day to day—and employee turnover in a retail outlet like Mrs. Fields is high—it makes sense to run basic store operations as close to autopilot as possible. But most larger companies compete in more dynamic environments than Mrs. Fields, and, therefore, a corporate business model must do more than connect hardwired processes. It must also specify the roles and accountabilities of the people involved, incorporate the unplanned activity that can take up to 80% of a working day, and build in sufficient latitude for individual decision-making.

Institutionalizing Flexibility

Large organizations have become too complex for any individual, even the most brilliant executive, to keep complete models of the business in mind. Whether individually or collectively, managers of companies with hundreds of millions in revenue and tens of thousands of employees can't track everything that happens, much less coordinate millions of elements into a timely, coherent response. In fact, they never could, which is why functional hierarchies were originally created.

The old chain of command was designed for a relatively stable—and now increasingly rare—make-and-sell business. But many fast-growing sense-and-respond companies never adopted functional hierarchies in the first place. Instead, in the process of expanding, they have used IT-enabled networks as the tendons that hold the skeleton and muscles of the company together. Large companies, attempting to compete with agile niche players, are heading in the opposite direction of hardwiring operations. Rather than explicitly specifying "do it this way," many executives are empowering employees to "do it the best way you know how." However, without coordination, accountability, and shared objectives, this approach can often lead to paralysis rather than coherent companywide behavior.

The need for flexibility drove the $1 billion utility, Brooklyn Union Gas of New York, to a radically different IT strategy. By the early 1980s, Brooklyn Union's 1971 Customer-Related Information System (CRIS) had become obsolete. Among other things, the Public Service Commission had begun requiring utilities to treat certain customers—for example, the elderly and disabled—in different ways. Top-level executives were also convinced that micromarketing increasingly customized service offerings was essential to Brooklyn Union's competitive survival. But the practices and policies of 1971 had become petrified in software procedures that were finally rendered obsolete by the dynamic environment that the company faced in the 1980s.

A $2 million initial attempt to upgrade CRIS failed. Finally, after spending more than three years on feasibility studies, design, and prototype systems, senior

management agreed to let the IT department completely redo CRIS. The project began in the spring of
1987 and was completed by January 1990 at a cost of
$48 million. In this case, the manage-by-wire imple-
mentation resulted not from a new business design by
management but from the system being redesigned by
a talented group of IT professionals.

The IT department chose to implement the new system using object-oriented programming. Objects are
reusable software building blocks: sets of instructions
that programmers can reassemble for a variety of different operations. CRIS now contains 650 such objects that
create, in various combinations, 10,000 appropriate
actions in 800 distinct business situations. These actions
cover everything from meter reading and cash processing to collection, billing, credit, and field service orders.
Brooklyn Union has now codified a substantial part of
its customer-related business behavior in these software
combinations. And because of the IT department's flexible, building-block approach to software, the system is
much easier to modify than a hardwired one.

But at Brooklyn Union, as at Mrs. Fields, the IT
department functions as the intermediary between customer-related management policy and its execution. The
IT shop translates into software an understanding of
management's business changes. It does this by defining
the conditions that dictate legitimate combinations of
software objects. These conditions may relate to business policy, legal requirements, or common-sense logic:
for example, "You can't cut off service to an elderly customer before x months," or "You can't bill a customer if
you haven't installed a meter."

Brooklyn Union exemplifies how computers can be
used to create and manage building blocks of business

activity that can then be combined and recombined into a variety of responses. However, senior executives are still disconnected from direct influence over the software that determines how their company handles customers. In fact, it is middle managers, rather than senior executives, who are managing by wire. And in the sense that the IT department acts as intermediary, Brooklyn Union has not moved beyond the practices of many large companies.

Not that top management at Brooklyn Union feels shortchanged. Its IT experts had the vision and ability to build in exceptional flexibility by using object-oriented software. As a result, new capabilities can now be created by extensively reusing existing software objects and adding only those required for specific additional functions. A proposal for a new engineering system, for instance, estimated that up to 30% of the software objects that were required to implement the system already existed in CRIS. More important, CRIS has delivered on top management's mandate against obsolescence, allowing Brooklyn Union to respond to market change and new opportunities in a timely way and at a reasonable cost.

Creating an Enterprise Model of a Business

Mrs. Fields's and Brooklyn Union's IT strategies demonstrate that manage-by-wire implementations vary from business to business, depending on size and complexity. A company's complexity is a function of how many information sources it needs, how many business elements it must coordinate, and the number and type of relationships that exist among those elements. We think of a company's *corporate IQ* as its institutional ability to deal with complexity, that is, its ability to capture, share, and extract meaning from marketplace signals. Corporate IQ directly translates into three IT infrastructure imperatives for connecting, sharing, and structuring information (see the chart "How 'Smart' Is a Company in a Complex World?").

In most large companies, a low IQ results from change occurring so rapidly that keeping computer applications up to date is neither feasible nor affordable. Low IQs are particularly prevalent when processes have been automated over decades without any framework to integrate disparate applications and databases. At Mrs. Fields, where there are few information sources and clear and unchanging employee roles, ROI creates a high corporate IQ in an environment of comparatively low complexity.

Neither Mrs. Fields nor Brooklyn Union has a coherent model that fully maps key business processes.

How "Smart" is a Company in a Complex World?

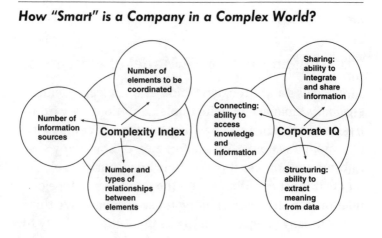

Brooklyn Union's CRIS is less complete because it captures a smaller percentage of the total business. But this larger company operates in a much more complex industry. Brooklyn Union has a high capacity for sharing information and a comprehensive knowledge base in one important area: customers. Compared with many other large companies—with their disconnected information systems, competing computer platforms, and ill-defined business processes—Brooklyn Union Gas looks like a corporate genius.

But neither Mrs. Fields nor Brooklyn Union has a coherent model that fully maps key processes, how information is interpreted, and who is accountable for what. It is just such a model that can replace the IT department as the intermediary between management policy and execution. In fact, large companies need a coherent enterprise model to raise their corporate IQ.

An enterprise model is a high-level map of a business that guides the writing of computer code and the execution of nonautomated activities. Once procedures, data flows, and employee accountabilities are represented in computers by specific bit patterns and machine states, the map becomes the terrain; in other words, it becomes "real" in cyberspace, that computer-generated realm in which the informational representations of a cookie store or a utility's customer-related activities can be manipulated and modified. Companies can use an enterprise model to leverage a computer's memory and speed; to track and interrelate millions of events and relationships simultaneously; to allow selective sharing of information; and, finally, to initiate physical processes.

Of course, enterprise modeling tools have been available from software consultants and vendors for more than 25 years. Used primarily by information systems professionals to lay out procedures and data flows for certain business operations, the first generation of these tools were essentially high-level flow charts. Useful in highlighting procedural redundancies and omissions, they nonetheless have several major drawbacks that prevented their widespread adoption by management for designing business functions:

- They fail to incorporate the notions of commitment and human accountability in business processes, a particularly important omission because procedure without accountability often leads to bureaucracy.

- They don't deal with unstructured work and ad hoc processes.

- They take years to map into computer code, by which time the model is badly out of date.

Clearly, corporate managers, not IT professionals, should design a business. And business design extends beyond procedural design; it includes making strategic decisions about what market signals should be sensed, what data or analytical models should be used to interpret those signals, and how an appropriate response should be executed. To faithfully represent management's design, a robust enterprise model must consistently characterize any process at any scale, exhaustively account for the possible outcomes of every process, and unambiguously specify the roles and accountabilities of the employees involved in carrying them out.

A new generation of enterprise modeling tools that overcomes the drawbacks of traditional modeling tools is now emerging. Admittedly, creating a comprehensive information map is no simple task, but the benefits can be substantial, even for small business units. In a test at a large manufacturing company, one of these new enterprise modeling tools was used to map an engineering change process for electronic circuitry. Senior executives considered this process among the best in the organization. However, the new modeling tool not only revealed opportunities for procedural improvements, such as removing manufacturing bottlenecks, it also uncovered this startling fact: during the entire operation, not one person in the entire organization made a single commitment on volumes, cost, or delivery dates—only forecasts, estimates, and targets. If accountability isn't specified, business processes lack discipline and predictability, making them difficult to manage. A model that defines both procedures *and* accountability for outcomes can help managers of large companies do the job of managing.

The new enterprise modeling tools, for example, could make a substantial difference at Brooklyn Union Gas. CRIS uses data models to interpret signals from meter readings, field reports, and cash receipts. But the utility company has yet to develop an enterprise model that allows top managers to define and modify the policies that determine permissible combinations of its reusable software objects. An enterprise model would raise Brooklyn Union's corporate IQ by enhancing the structure of its customer information system. In effect, top-level managers would move into the information cockpit and gain the ability to modify directly how CRIS drives customer-related activities.

Designing the Intelligent Corporation

To be useful in today's dynamic business environment, an enterprise model must do more than represent a static version of "how we do things around here"; it must also include the capacity to adapt systematically and rapidly. Like the process of piloting a jet fighter, a true manage-by-wire system relies both on an accurate information model and on the organization's ability to learn.

The United States Air Force assesses a pilot's ability to learn with the OODA Loop, a model for the mental processes of a fighter pilot. OODA stands for:

- **Observation:** sensing environmental signals;

- **Orientation:** interpreting those signals;

- **Decision:** selecting from a repertoire of available responses;

- **Action:** executing the response selected.

Fighter pilots with faster OODA Loops tend to win dogfights, while those with slower ones get more parachute practice. Note that the loop is iterative: a continuous cycle in which an action leads to the observation of the results of that action that in turn requires a new orientation, decision, and action. This iterative sequence constitutes a *learning loop*. It contains the four functions essential to any adaptive organism: sensing, interpreting, deciding, and acting. By analogy, an enterprise model for a business that incorporates learning is one that systematically creates and links learning loops (see the chart "Learning Loops").

Wal-Mart's learning loop lowers logistics and inventory costs and leads to fewer stock outs.

Recent work on organizational learning focuses on the way that people in a company learn. But what about *institutional* learning? How much do companies know when the people go home at night? Many companies, with the aid of software, would know how to process payrolls. Some would know how to dispense cash and others how to replenish stocks. But one could hardly call that learning.

We define institutional learning as the process by which information models change, be they data models, forecasting models, or procedural models. Therefore, a good enterprise model should include a design for systematically chang-ing these kinds of mod-els, based on signals received from the envi-ronment. That means an adaptive organization avoids running learning loops repeatedly over static informa-tion models.

An intelligent company integrates "what's going on out there" with "how we do things around here."

An example of an institutional learning loop at work is the system that Wal-Mart and its apparel suppliers use to replenish stocks in Wal-Mart stores. For instance,

Learning Loops

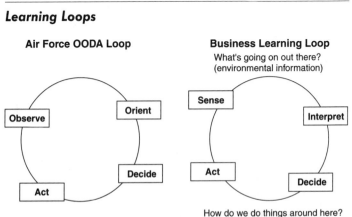

Air Force OODA Loop

Observe
Orient
Decide
Act

Business Learning Loop
What's going on out there?
(environmental information)

Sense
Interpret
Act
Decide

How do we do things around here?
(business processes)

every evening, Wal-Mart transmits five million charac-
ters of data about the day's sales to Wrangler, a supplier
of blue jeans. The two companies share both the data
and a model that interprets the meaning of the data.
They also share software applications that act on that
interpretation to send specific quantities of specific sizes
and colors of jeans to specific stores from specific warehouses. The result is a learning loop that lowers logistics
and inventory costs and leads to fewer stock outs. And
every time the data model is changed to reflect a new
fashion season or pricing pattern, both Wal-Mart and
Wrangler learn and adapt.

Using technology to integrate how an organization
interprets "what's going on out there" with a codification
of "how we do things around here" creates an intelligent
corporation. The company we call Global Insurance (the
real company is disguised) is one of the best examples of
managing by wire at this level of sophistication.

A large financial services organization, Global was
driven to a fundamental reconceptualization of how it
does business because of competition from niche players in the 1980s. The $78 billion company was facing
extinction. New policies took two years from concep-
tion to consumer, and operational costs were 15%
higher than those of smaller competitors, who were
luring customers away with innovative offerings. Fur-
thermore, the insurance industry was changing so
rapidly that senior executives had little confidence that
any specific strategy would keep the company afloat
for more than a year or two.

In the late 1980s, rather than investing in a specific
business strategy, top-level managers decided to spend
$110 million on an IT infrastructure that would allow
them to implement *any* strategy quickly. Senior execu-

tives started the project with the development of an enterprise model for the company's two largest business lines: casualty and life insurance. The model linked product development, underwriting, sales, and other functions in a coherent informational representation of "how we do things around here." Information specialists created the model based on senior managers' specifications of the information they wanted to track (observation); the data models needed to interpret the information (orientation); the analytic and decision support provided for underwriters, actuaries, and managers in the field (decision); and, finally, how these decisions should be executed via their on-line transaction systems (action).

Elaborate data models are worth fortunes to banks, airlines, food manufacturers, and large retailers.

Using combinations of more than 1,000 software objects, the company created the transactions, activities, and data that would, when properly linked, define any present or future offering in its life- or casualty-insurance business lines. "Enroll client," "send premium notice," and "establish risk limit" are examples of these software building blocks.

In addition, data models were developed to interpret the market research, transaction history, demographic, and economic information that Global collected from the field, external databases, and internal operations. Data models are explicit renderings of the way an application program, or a collection of these programs, views the world. When these models are used to create databases, they institutionalize specific ways of interpreting raw data. Elaborate data models are worth fortunes to banks, airlines, food manufacturers, and large retailers like Wal-Mart, because they help these companies reorient themselves continually.

At Global, a decision-support system used the patterns its data models revealed to trigger exception reports or approval requests that then appeared on managers' terminals. For instance, a manager whose product was losing ground to a new competitive offering would have the option of modifying the existing policy or creating an entirely new one. This process was codified by expert systems that contain legal, logical, and business constraints: for example, "we will not underwrite an aggregate risk for a single client that is more than x times the client's net worth."

Through this manage-by-wire capability, decision-to-action times have been reduced by 400% to 700%, enabling Global to meet the competition of small niche players. And certain types of decisions can now be carried out in real time. One example: agents, who have their own laptop computers with easy access to Global's electronic network, can customize a policy in a client's living room. They can tailor policies based on a client's specific situation, such as annual income, ages of dependents, or lifestyle preferences.

There was, of course, substantial technological risk associated with Global's project. Still riskier was counting on the ability of managers to specify adequately the hundreds of procedures and dozens of management policies necessary to ensure that Global's responses were consistent with its business goals. The CEO also worried that his information systems team, lacking sufficient business experience, might misinterpret these specifications when they translated business rules into the language of data models and expert systems. It was only through extensive prototyping that senior executives acquired the confidence to transfer processes gradually to the manage-by-wire system.

Along the way, Global has experienced setbacks. Vendor technology was late and slow. Some managers, who implicitly relied on bureaucratic procedures to buffer them from direct accountability for policy changes, resisted the extensive retraining that was designed to put them in the pilot's seat. In fact, many managers didn't make the shift successfully. Some key executives retired or left the company, taking with them crucial knowledge that the rest of the institution hadn't learned because it had never been codified.

But after more than a year's delay and a budgetary overrun, Global has implemented almost all it set out to do technologically. Because its enterprise model wasn't developed with the new generation of modeling tools, changes to the model must still be made by the IT shop. Still, the senior executives who run the life and casualty businesses are managing by wire a large portion of their operations. With a few additional changes, managers will be able to modify underwriting policy themselves through the IT system and have these changes reflected immediately in the policies written by agents.

Setting Guidelines for Managing by Wire

Given the right enterprise model and a technology-enabled capacity to learn, a large company's size can again become a decisive competitive advantage. But to many managers, Global Insurance's successful manage-by-wire strategy will seem unattainable. For one thing, the technical expertise needed to implement such an integrated system may not exist within the company. The ability to change reality by modifying an informational representation of it is possible only with an underlying technological infrastructure that has a high corporate IQ. Indeed, managing by wire requires the long-term commitment of both senior executives *and* a world-class IT group.

Flying a modern jet airplane is a sophisticated operation. The current generation of fly-by-wire systems requires more than 20 million lines of computer code. Yet if an aviation information model can successfully capture this level of complexity, an enterprise model can do the same for the managers of rapidly changing business units. In fact, adopting a manage-by-wire strategy is nothing less than a change in the nature of strategy itself, from a *plan* to produce specific offerings for specific markets to a *structure* for sensing and responding to change faster than the competition.

Managers must shift from a plan to produce specific offerings for specific markets to a structure for responding to change.

Faced with an unpredictable business environment, top managers at Global Insurance were forced to fuse their business and IT strategies. It's imperative that today's senior executives make IT policy an integral part of corporate strategy and intent. Technological knowledge must join the financial and operational know-how of a policy-making manager; otherwise, crucial business decisions will implicitly be delegated to the IT department.

Managers can follow a few guidelines to help them implement a manage-by-wire system:

Top managers must assess a company's corporate IQ in terms of connecting, sharing, and structuring information. There are three critical attributes of a company's IT infrastructure that determine its corporate IQ. *Connecting* means the degree to which the IT platform links information sources, media, locations, and users. Since the 1970s, computer networks have sprung up in multiple places for multiple purposes. As a result, many companies today are crisscrossed by dozens of independent networks that are incompatible technically and thus actually inhibit, rather than promote, information sharing. Mere connectivity doesn't necessarily increase productivity *or* institutional learning. Management must not only determine what the signals should be but also ensure that these signals are understood and shared by the right people and teams.

Sharing makes possible coordinated effort and, therefore, the benefits associated with teamwork, integration, and extended scope. Getting everyone on the same page in a large business requires an institutional capability to share data, interpretations of that data, and specifications of core processes. The added value that this integration can yield underlines a subtle but important distinction: the actual implementation of a breakthrough application, such as an automated airline reservation system like American Airlines's SABRE, may ultimately be less important than *how* that application is implemented. A stand-alone application is less likely to deliver sustainable competitive advantage than one implemented on an integrated technology platform designed for extensive information sharing. Anyone who receives multiple premium notices on the same day from the same insurance company for different policies is on the receiving end of an unintegrated IT platform.

Structuring holds the most potential for the strategic exploitation of information in the 1990s and beyond. Structure is created by information about information, for instance, how data is classified, organized, related, and used. Tables of contents, indices, and "see also" references are familiar hard-copy examples. The data models of Global Insurance and Wal-Mart structure information by filtering the data that bombards these companies every day.

When information from previously unrelated sources is structured in a meaningful way, human beings become capable of thinking thoughts that were previously unthinkable. Computers that use their speed and memory to reveal patterns in raw data augment the extraordinary capacity of humans to recognize and assign meaning to patterns. For example, through spectral analysis and mathematical equations that model what scientists call the red shift, a computer can process light signals from a remote galaxy to calculate the distance and size of its parts. The results can be displayed in a three-dimensional picture and then rotated. Presentation in this manner allows scientists to "see" a distant galaxy from the back or side and even to discover, as they did recently, a huge void passing through it.

An enterprise model should be expressed in business language, not IT terminology. Management should select and use one business design language and insist on its use throughout the organization. In many companies, a variety of first- and second-generation enterprise modeling tools have already been used to capture key processes in different functions or operating units. But in order to create a unified understanding of "how we do things around here" (and, if it makes strategic sense, to facilitate future integration of presently autonomous organizational units), a common business language is required.

Senior executives must determine the highest level at which coherent institutional behavior adds value. Managers must decide which business units, if well coordinated, could together create more value than the sum of their individual parts. In many respects, this is the strategic task facing managers in a sense-and-respond world. There's no one answer to this crucial issue. Many different approaches have been tried, even in an information-intensive industry like publishing. McGraw Hill's strategy, for example, is to treat their information systems and certain editorial content as assets to be shared among multiple units. Dun and Bradstreet, on the other hand, views its information and technology as assets to be separated into individual units. In other words, McGraw Hill shares assets at the enterprise level and Dun and Bradstreet at the business-line level.

Once a company embarks on a manage-by-wire strategy, senior executives must carefully plan the pace of its implementation. Just as information technology has fueled a new competitive dynamic for businesses, the advent of jet-engine technology in the 1950s profoundly affected aviation. By increasing the speed of fighter planes, the jet engine made it impossible for pilots to fly planes manually. But flying by wire didn't happen overnight. In the mid-1950s, no pilot would have felt safe with a sudden and comprehensive introduction of software between the cockpit controls and the physical airplane, even if the technology had existed at the time. In fact, only the latest generation of commercial aircraft truly fly by wire.

Similarly, few executives will feel confident enough to commit their company to managing by wire in one

massive effort. How fast and how far they're willing to go
will depend on how effectively the software currently
mediates management decisions; how much confidence
managers have in their IT staff; and how much money
and time it will ultimately take to implement the process.

When a target level for coherent institutional behavior
has been defined, common information and technology
assets can be leveraged to create economies of scope. But
realistically, most companies will model smaller business
domains first, such as Brooklyn Union's customer information system. They will then link these domains to
cover larger parts of the business, as Global did.

No corporation has implemented a fully integrated
manage-by-wire system yet. But a growing number of
companies like Brooklyn Union Gas and Global Insurance are showing that large and complicated business
operations can be captured in an information technology structure and used to govern business behavior.
These companies have already significantly improved
their response times and substantially reduced the costs
of developing new products and services.

The imminent arrival of a new generation of enterprise modeling tools makes a manage-by-wire strategy
plausible. But it will be management's skill in codifying a
competitive information model that will determine its
success.

Originally published in September–October 1993
Reprint 93503

*The description of CRIS and its management implications has benefited
from discussions with Joe Pinnola and Tom Morgan of Brooklyn Union*

Gas and Ben Konsynski of Emory University, who has written a Harvard Business School case study on Brooklyn Union, "Brooklyn Union Gas: OOPS on Big Iron." In addition, we have based our discussion of new enterprise modeling tools on Alan Scherr's work at IBM, which is described in his article, "A New Approach to Business Processes" (IBM Systems Journal, February 1993).

Putting the Enterprise into the Enterprise System

THOMAS H. DAVENPORT

Executive Summary

ENTERPRISE SYSTEMS PRESENT A NEW model of corporate computing. They allow companies to replace their existing information systems, which are often incompatible with one another, with a single, integrated system. By streamlining data flows throughout an organization, these commercial software packages, offered by vendors like SAP, promise dramatic gains in a company's efficiency and bottom line. It's no wonder that businesses are rushing to jump on the ES bandwagon.

But while these systems offer tremendous rewards, the risks they carry are equally great. Not only are the systems expensive and difficult to implement, they can also tie the hands of managers. Unlike computer systems of the past, which were typically developed in-house with a company's specific requirements in mind, enterprise systems are off-the-shelf solutions. They impose their own logic on a company's strategy, culture, and organization, often forcing companies to change the way they do business. Managers would do well to heed the horror stories of failed implementations. FoxMeyer Drug, for example, claims that its system helped drive it into bankruptcy.

Drawing on examples of both successful and unsuccessful ES projects, the author discusses the pros and cons of implementing an enterprise system, showing how a system can produce unintended and highly disruptive consequences. Because of an ES's profound business implications, he cautions against shifting responsibility for its adoption to technologists. Only a general manager will be able to mediate between the imperatives of the system and the imperatives of the business.

ENTERPRISE SYSTEMS APPEAR to be a dream come true. These commercial software packages promise the seamless integration of all the information flowing through a company—financial and accounting information, human resource information, supply chain information, customer information. For managers who have struggled, at great expense and with great frustration, with incompatible information systems and inconsistent operating practices, the promise of an off-the-shelf solution to the problem of business integration is enticing.

The growing number of horror stories about failed or out-of-control projects should certainly give managers pause.

It comes as no surprise, then, that companies have been beating paths to the doors of enterprise-system developers. The sales of the largest vendor, Germany's SAP, have soared from less than $500 million in 1992 to approximately $3.3 billion in 1997, making it the fastest-growing software company in the world. SAP's competitors, including such companies as Baan, Oracle, and PeopleSoft, have also seen rapid growth in demand for their packages. It is estimated that businesses around the world are now spending $10 billion per year on enterprise systems—also commonly referred to as enterprise resource planning, or ERP, systems—and that figure probably doubles when you add in associated consulting expenditures. While the rise of the Internet has received most of the media attention in recent years, the business world's embrace of enterprise systems may in fact be the most important development in the corporate use of information technology in the 1990s.

An enterprise system imposes its own logic on a company's strategy, culture, and organization.

But are enterprise systems living up to companies' expectations? The growing number of horror stories about failed or out-of-control projects should certainly give managers pause. FoxMeyer Drug argues that its system helped drive it into bankruptcy. Mobil Europe spent hundreds of millions of dollars on its system only to abandon it when its merger partner objected. Dell Computer found that its system would not fit its new, decentralized management model. Applied Materials gave up on its system when it found itself overwhelmed by the organizational changes involved. Dow Chemical spent seven years and close to half a billion dollars implementing a mainframe-based enterprise system; now it has decided to start over again on a client-server version.

Some of the blame for such debacles lies with the enormous technical challenges of rolling out enterprise systems—these systems are profoundly complex pieces of software, and installing them requires large investments of money, time, and expertise. But the technical challenges, however

Enterprise systems can deliver great rewards, but the risks they carry are equally great.

great, are not the main reason enterprise systems fail. The biggest problems are business problems. Companies fail to reconcile the technological imperatives of the enterprise system with the business needs of the enterprise itself.

An enterprise system, by its very nature, imposes its own logic on a company's strategy, organization, and culture. (See the table "The Scope of an Enterprise System.") It pushes a company toward full integration even when a certain degree of business-unit segregation may be in its best interests. And it pushes a company toward generic processes even when customized processes may be a source of competitive advantage. If a company rushes to install an enterprise system without first having a clear understanding of the business implications, the dream of integration can quickly turn into a nightmare. The logic of the system may conflict with the logic of the business, and either the implementation will fail, wasting vast sums of money and causing a great deal of disruption, or the system will weaken important sources of competitive advantage, hobbling the company.

The Scope of an Enterprise System

An enterprise system enables a company to integrate the data used throughout its entire organization. This list shows some of the many functions supported by SAP's R/3 package.

Financials
Accounts receivable and payable
Asset accounting
Cash management and forecasting
Cost-element and cost-center accounting
Executive information system
Financial consolidation
General ledger
Product-cost accounting
Profitability analysis
Profit-center accounting
Standard and period-related costing

Human Resources
Human-resources time accounting
Payroll
Personnel planning
Travel expenses

Operations and Logistics
Inventory management
Material requirements planning
Materials management
Plant maintenance
Production planning
Project management
Purchasing
Quality management
Routing management
Shipping
Vendor evaluation

Sales and Marketing
Order management
Pricing
Sales management
Sales planning

It is certainly true that enterprise systems can deliver great rewards, but the risks they carry are equally great. When considering and implementing an enterprise system, managers need to be careful that their enthusiasm about the benefits does not blind them to the hazards.

The Allure of Enterprise Systems

In order to understand the attraction of enterprise systems, as well as their potential dangers, you first need to understand the problem they're designed to solve: the fragmentation of information in large business organizations. Every big company collects, generates, and stores vast quantities of data. In most companies, though, the data are not kept in a single repository. Rather, the information is spread across dozens or even hundreds of separate computer systems, each housed in an individual function, business unit, region, factory, or office. Each of these so-called legacy systems may provide invaluable support for a particular business activity. But in combination, they represent one of the heaviest drags on business productivity and performance now in existence.

Maintaining many different computer systems leads to enormous costs—for storing and rationalizing redundant data, for rekeying and reformatting data from one system for use in another, for updating and debugging obsolete software code, for programming communication links between systems to automate the transfer of data. But even more important than the direct costs are the indirect ones. If a company's sales and ordering systems cannot talk with its production-scheduling systems, then its manufacturing productivity and customer responsiveness suffer. If its sales and marketing systems are incompatible with its financial-reporting systems, then management is left to make important decisions by instinct rather than according to a detailed understanding of product and customer profitability. To put it bluntly: if a company's systems are fragmented, its business is fragmented.

Enter the enterprise system. A good ES is a technological tour de force. At its core is a single comprehensive database. The database collects data from and feeds data into modular applications supporting virtually all of a company's business activities—across functions, across business units, across the world. (See the chart "Anatomy of an Enterprise System.") When new information is entered in one place, related information is automatically updated.

Let's say, for example, that a Paris-based sales representative for a U.S. computer manufacturer prepares a quote for a customer using an ES. The salesperson enters some basic information about the customer's requirements into his laptop computer, and the ES automatically produces a formal contract, in French, specifying the product's configuration, price, and delivery date. When the customer accepts the quote, the sales rep hits a key; the system, after verifying the customer's credit limit, records the order. The system schedules the shipment; identifies the best routing; and then, working backward from the delivery date, reserves the necessary materials from inventory; orders needed parts from suppliers; and schedules assembly in the company's factory in Taiwan.

The sales and production forecasts are immediately updated, and a material-requirements-planning list and bill of materials are created. The sales rep's payroll account is credited with the correct commission, in French francs, and his travel account is credited with the expense of the sales call. The actual product cost and profitability are calculated, in U.S. dollars, and the divisional and corporate balance sheets, the accounts-payable and accounts-receivable ledgers, the cost-center accounts, and the corporate cash levels are all automatically updated. The system performs nearly every information transaction resulting from the sale.

An ES streamlines a company's data flows and provides management with direct access to a wealth of real-time operating information. For many companies, these benefits have translated into dramatic gains in productivity and speed.

Anatomy of an Enterprise System

At the heart of an enterprise system is a central database that draws data from and feeds data into a series of applications supporting diverse company functions. Using a single database dramatically streamlines the flow of information throughout a business.

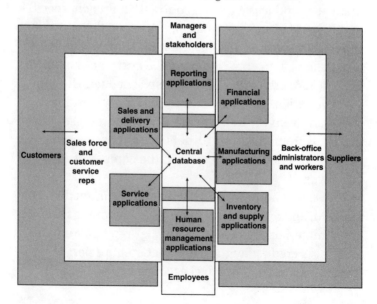

Autodesk, a leading maker of computer-aided design software, used to take an average of two weeks to deliver an order to a customer. Now, having installed an ES, it ships 98% of its orders within 24 hours. IBM's Storage Systems division reduced the time required to reprice all of its products from 5 days to 5 minutes, the time to ship a replacement part from 22 days to 3 days, and the time to complete a credit check from 20 minutes to 3 seconds. Fujitsu Microelectronics reduced the cycle time for filling orders from 18 days to a day and a half and cut the time required to close its financial books from 8 days to 4 days.

When System and Strategy Clash

Clearly, enterprise systems offer the potential of big benefits. But the very quality of the systems that makes those benefits possible—their almost universal applicability—also presents a danger. When developing information systems in the past, companies would first decide how they wanted to do business and then choose a software package that would support their proprietary processes. They often rewrote large portions of the software code to ensure a tight fit. With enterprise systems, however, the sequence is reversed. The business often must be modified to fit the system.

An enterprise system is, after all, a generic solution. Its design reflects a series of assumptions about the way companies operate in general. Vendors try to structure the systems to reflect best practices, but it is the vendor, not the customer, that is defining what "best" means. In many cases, the system will enable a company to operate more efficiently than it did before. In some cases, though, the system's assumptions will run counter to a company's best interests.

Some degree of ES customization is possible. Because the systems are modular, for instance, companies can install only those modules that are most appropriate to their business. However, the system's complexity makes major modifications impracticable. (See "Configuring an Enterprise System" on page 183.) As a result, most companies installing enterprise systems will need to adapt or even completely rework their processes to fit the requirements of the system. An executive of one company that has adopted SAP's system sums it up by saying, "SAP isn't a software package; it's a way of doing business." The question is, Is it the best way of doing business? Do the system's technical imperatives coincide or conflict with the company's business imperatives?

Imagine, for example, an industrial products manufacturer that has built its strategy around its ability to provide extraordinary customer service in filling orders for spare parts. Because it is able to consistently deliver parts to customers 25% faster than its competitors—often by circumventing formal processes and systems—it has gained a large and loyal clientele who are happy to pay a premium price for its products. If, after installing an ES, the company has to follow a more rational but less flexible process for filling orders, its core source of advantage may be at risk. The company may integrate its data and improve its processes only to lose its service edge and, in turn, its customers.

This danger becomes all the more pressing in light of the increasing ubiquity of enterprise systems. It is now common for a single ES package to be used by virtually every company in an industry. For example, SAP's R/3 package is being implemented by almost every company in the personal computer, semiconductor, petrochemical, and to a slightly lesser degree, consumer goods industries. (R/3 is the client-server version of SAP's software; R/2 is the mainframe version.) Such convergence around a single software package should raise a sobering question in the minds of chief executives: How similar can our information flows and our processes be to those of our competitors before we begin to undermine our own sources of differentiation in the market?

This question will be moot if a company's competitive advantage derives primarily from the distinctiveness of its products. Apple Computer, for example, has many problems, but the loss of competitive differentiation because of its ES is not one of them. With a strong brand and a unique operating system, its computers still differ dramatically from competing offerings. But Apple is an unusual case. Among most makers of personal computers, differentiation is based more on service and price than on product. For those companies, there is a very real risk that an enterprise system could dissolve their sources of advantage.

Compaq Computer is a good example of a company that carefully thought through the strategic implications of implementing an enterprise system. Like many personal-computer companies, Compaq had decided to shift from a build-to-stock to a build-to-order business model. Because the success of a build-to-order model hinges on the speed with which information flows through a company, Compaq believed that a fully integrated enterprise system was essential. At the same time, however, Compaq saw the danger in adopting processes indistinguishable from those of its competitors.

It realized, in particular, that in a build-to-order environment an important advantage would accrue to any company with superior capabilities for forecasting demand and processing orders. Compaq therefore decided to invest in writing its own proprietary applications to support its forecasting and order-management processes. To ensure that those applications would be compatible with its ES, Compaq wrote them in the computer language used by its ES vendor.

Compaq's course was not the obvious one. It cost the company considerably more to develop the proprietary application modules than it would have to use the modules offered by the ES vendor. And using customized applications meant forgoing some of the integration benefits of a pure enterprise system. But Compaq saw the decision as a strategic necessity: it was the only way to protect a potentially critical source of advantage.

For companies that compete on cost rather than on distinctive products or superior customer service, enterprise systems raise different strategic issues. The huge investment required to implement an ES at large companies—typically ranging from $50 million to more than $500 million—need to be weighed carefully against the eventual savings the system will produce. In some cases, companies may find that by forgoing an ES they can actually gain a cost advantage over competitors that are embracing the systems. They may not have the most elegant computer system or the most integrated information flows and processes, but if customers are concerned only with price, that may not matter.

Air Products and Chemicals, for example, saw that many of its competitors were installing large, complex enterprise systems. After a thorough evaluation, it decided not to follow their lead. Its managers reasoned that the cost of an ES might force the company to raise its prices, leading to lost sales in some of the commodity gas markets in which it competes. The company's existing systems, while not state-of-the-art, were adequate to meet its needs. And since the company had no plans to exchange information electronically with competitors, it didn't worry about being the odd man out in its industry.

Of course, the long-term productivity and connectivity gains created by enterprise systems are often so compelling that not adopting one is out of the question. In the petrochemicals industry, for example, enterprise systems have improved the flow of information through the supply chain to such a degree that they have become a de facto operating standard. Because participants in the industry routinely share information electronically, it would today be hard for a company to survive in the business without an ES. Still, the cost of implementation should be a primary concern. It will often be in a company's interest to go ahead and rework its processes to fit the system requirements. The alternative—customizing the system to fit the processes or writing proprietary application modules—will simply be too expensive to justify. As the CEO of one large chemical firm says, "Competitive advantage in this industry might just come from doing the best and cheapest job at implementing SAP."

The Impact on an Organization

In addition to having important strategic implications, enterprise systems also have a direct, and often paradoxical, impact on a company's organization and culture. On the one hand, by providing universal, real-time access to operating and financial data, the systems allow companies to streamline their management structures, creating flatter, more flexible, and more democratic organizations. On the other hand, they also involve the centralization of control over information and the standardization of processes, which are qualities more consistent with hierarchical, command-and-control organizations with uniform cultures. In fact, it can be argued that the reason enterprise systems first emerged in Europe is that European companies tend to have more rigid, centralized organizational structures than their U.S. counterparts.

Some executives, particularly those in fast-growing high-tech companies, have used enterprise systems to inject more discipline into their organizations. They see the systems as a lever for exerting more management control and imposing more-uniform processes on free-wheeling, highly entrepreneurial cultures. An executive at a semiconductor company, for example, says, "We plan to use SAP as a battering ram to make our culture less autonomous." The manager of the ES implementation at a computer company expresses a similar thought: "We've had a renegade culture in the past, but our new system's going to make everybody fall into line."

But some companies have the opposite goal. They want to use their enterprise systems to break down hierarchical structures, freeing their people to be more innovative and more flexible. Take Union Carbide. Like most companies implementing enterprise systems, Union Carbide is standardizing its basic business transactions. Unlike many other companies, however, the leaders of its ES project are already thinking in depth about how the company will be managed differently when the project is completed. They plan to give low-level managers, workers, and even customers and suppliers much broader access to operating information. Standardizing transactions will make Union Carbide more efficient; sharing real-time information will make it more creative.

For a multinational corporation, enterprise systems raise another important organizational question: How much uniformity should exist in the way it does business in different regions or countries? Some big companies have used their enterprise systems to introduce more consistent operating practices across their geographically dispersed units. Dow Chemical, for instance, became an early convert to enterprise systems because it saw them as a way to cut costs by streamlining global financial and administrative processes. (A good idea in principle, although it became much more expensive to achieve than Dow had anticipated.) Some large manufacturers have been even more ambitious, using the systems as the basis for introducing a global lean-production model. By imposing common operating processes on all units, they are able to achieve tight coordination throughout their businesses. They can rapidly shift sourcing, manufacturing, and distribution functions worldwide in response to changing patterns of supply and demand. This capability allows them to minimize excess manufacturing capacity and reduce both component and finished-goods inventory.

Owens Corning, for example, adopted an ES to replace 211 legacy systems. For the company to grow internationally, its chief executive, Glen Hiner, felt it was critical to coordinate order-management, financial-reporting, and supply chain processes across the world. Having implemented the system and established a new global-procurement organization, the company is now able to enter into larger, more advantageous international contracts for supplies. Finished-goods inventory can be tracked daily, both in company warehouses and in the distribution channel, and spare-parts inventory has been reduced by 50%. The company expects to save $65 million by the end of 1998 as a result of its adoption of these globally coordinated processes.

For most companies, however, differences in regional markets remain so profound that strict process uniformity would be counterproductive. If companies in such circumstances don't allow their regional units to tailor their operations to local customer requirements and regulatory strictures, they risk sacrificing key markets to more flexible competitors. To preserve local autonomy while maintaining a degree of corporate control—what might be called a federalist operating model—a very different approach to enterprise systems needs to be taken. Rather than implement a single, global ES, these companies need to roll out different versions of the same system in each regional unit, tailored to support local operating practices. This approach has been taken by a number of large companies, including Hewlett-Packard, Monsanto, and Nestlé. They establish a core of common information—financial, say—that all units share, but they allow other information—on customers, say—to be collected, stored, and controlled locally. This method of implementation trades off some of the purity and simplicity of the enterprise system for greater market responsiveness.

The federalist model raises what is perhaps the most difficult challenge for a manager implementing an ES: determining what should be common throughout the organization and what should be allowed to vary. Corporate and business-unit managers will need to sit down together—well before system implementation begins—to think through each major type of information and each major process in the company. Difficult questions need to be raised: How important is it for us to process orders in a consistent manner worldwide? Does the term "customer" mean the same thing in every business unit? Answering such questions is essential to making an ES successful.

Different companies will, of course, reach very different decisions about the right balance between commonality and variability. Consider the starkly different approaches taken by Monsanto and Hewlett-Packard. Monsanto's managers knew that different operating requirements would preclude the complete standardization of data across its agrochemical, biotechnology, and pharmaceuticals businesses. Nevertheless, they placed a high priority on achieving the greatest possible degree of commonality. After studying the data requirements of each business unit, Monsanto's managers were able to standardize fully 85% of the data used in the ES. The company went from using 24 coding schemes for suppliers to using just one, and it standardized all data about materials using a new set of substance identification codes. While customer and factory data have not been fully standardized—differences among the units' customers and manufacturing processes are too great to accommodate common data—Monsanto has achieved a remarkable degree of commonality across a diverse set of global businesses.

Those companies that stressed the enterprise, not the system, gained the greatest benefits.

At Hewlett-Packard, a company with a strong tradition of business-unit autonomy, management has not pushed for commonality across the several large divisions that are implementing SAP's enterprise system. Except for a small amount of common financial data necessary to roll up results for corporate reporting, HP's federalist approach gives all the power to the "states" where ES decisions are concerned. This approach fits the HP culture well, but it's very expensive. Each divisional ES has had to be implemented separately, with little sharing of resources. Managers estimate that well over a billion dollars will be spent across the corporation before the various projects are completed.

Doing It Right at Elf Atochem

Considering an ES's far-reaching strategic and organizational implications, the worst thing a company can do is to make decisions about a system based on technical criteria alone. In fact, having now studied more than 50 businesses with enterprise systems, I can say with some confidence that the companies deriving the greatest benefits from their systems are those that, from the start, viewed them primarily in strategic and organizational terms. They stressed the *enterprise*, not the *system*.

Elf Atochem North America, a $2 billion regional chemicals subsidiary of the French company Elf Aquitaine, is a good case in point. Following a series of mergers in the early 1990s, Elf Atochem found itself hampered by the fragmentation of critical information systems among its 12 business units. Ordering systems were not integrated with production systems. Sales forecasts were not tied to budgeting systems or to performance-measurement systems. Each unit was tracking and reporting its financial data independently. As a result of the many incompatible systems, operating data were not flowing smoothly through the organization, and top management was not getting the information it needed to make sound and timely business decisions.

The company's executives saw that an enterprise system would be the best way to integrate the data flows, and they decided to go with SAP's R/3 system, which was rapidly becoming the standard in the industry. But they never labeled the ES project as simply a technology initiative. Rather, they viewed it as an opportunity to take a fresh look at the company's strategy and organization.

Looking beyond the technology, the executives saw that the real source of Elf Atochem's difficulties was not the fragmentation of its systems but the fragmentation of its organization. Although the 12 business units shared many of the same customers, each unit was managed autonomously. From the customer's perspective, the lack of continuity among units made doing business with the company a trial. To place a single order, a customer would frequently have to make many different phone calls to many different units. And to pay for the order, the customer would have to process a series of invoices.

Inside the company, things were equally confused. It took four days—and seven handoffs between departments—to process an order, even though only four hours of actual work were involved. Because each unit managed inventory and scheduled production independently, the company was unable to consolidate inventory or coordinate manufacturing at the corporate level. More than $6 million in inventory was written off every year, and plants had to be shut down frequently for unplanned production-line changes. And because ordering and production systems were not linked, sales representatives couldn't promise firm delivery dates, which translated into lost customers.

Management knew that in the petrochemicals business, where many products are commodities, the company that can offer the best customer service often wins the order. So it structured the implementation of its ES in a way that would enable it to radically improve its service levels. Its goal was to transform itself from an industry laggard into an industry leader. Even though many competitors were also adopting the R/3 package, Elf Atochem knew that if it could achieve a tighter, smoother fit between its business processes and the system, it could gain and maintain a service advantage.

The company decided to focus its efforts on four key processes: materials management, production planning, order management, and financial reporting. These cross-unit processes were the ones most distorted by the fragmented organizational structure. Moreover, they had the greatest impact on the company's ability to manage its customer relationships in a way that would both enhance customer satisfaction and improve corporate profitability. Each of the processes was redesigned to take full advantage of the new system's capabilities, in particular its ability to simplify the flow of information. Layers of information middlemen—once necessary for transferring information across incompatible unit and corporate systems—were eliminated in order to speed the flow of work and reduce the likelihood of errors.

To maintain its focus on the customer, the company chose to install only those R/3 modules required to support the four targeted processes. It did not, for example, install the modules for human resource management or plant maintenance. Those functions did not have a direct impact on customers, and the existing information systems that supported them were considered adequate.

Elf Atochem also made fundamental changes to its organizational structure. In the financial area, for example, all the company's accounts-receivable and credit departments were combined into a single corporate function. This change enabled the company to consolidate all of a customer's orders into a single account and issue a single invoice. It also allowed the company to monitor and manage overall customer profitability—something that had been impossible to do when orders were fragmented across units. In addition, Elf Atochem combined all of its units' customer-service departments into one department, providing each customer with a single point of contact for checking on orders and resolving problems.

Perhaps most important, the system gave Elf Atochem the real-time information it needed to connect sales and production planning—demand and supply—for the first time. As orders are entered or changed, the system automatically updates forecasts and factory schedules, which enables the company to quickly alter its production runs in response to customers needs. Only one other company in the industry had this capability, which meant that Elf Atochem gained an important edge over most competitors.

The company understood, however, that just having the data doesn't necessarily mean the data will be used well. Computer systems alone don't change organizational behavior. It therefore established a new position—demand manager—to be the focal point for the integrated sales and production-planning process. Drawing on the enterprise system, the demand manager creates the initial sales forecast, updates it with each new order, assesses plant capacity and account profitability, and develops detailed production plans. The demand manager is able to schedule a customer's order—and promise a delivery date—up to six weeks ahead of production. Previously, production could be allocated to individual orders no more than a week in advance. Now central to the company's operation, the role of demand manager could not even have existed in the past because the information needed to perform it was scattered all over the company.

The way Elf Atochem is managing the implementation effort also reflects the breadth of its goals. The project is being led by a 60-person core implementation team, which reports to a member of the company's executive committee. The team includes both business analysts and information technologists, and is assisted by a set of so-called super users, representing the business units and corporate functions. These super users help ensure that decisions about the system's configuration are made with the broadest possible understanding of the business. They also play a crucial role in explaining the new system to their respective departments and training people in its use.

The team is installing the ES one business unit at a time, with each unit implementing the same system configuration and set of procedures for order processing, supplier management, and financial reporting. The unit-by-unit process ensures that the effort is manageable, and it also helps the team refine the system and the processes as it proceeds. For example, the second unit to implement the system found that it didn't adequately support bulk shipments, which are the main way the unit gets its products to customers. (The first unit uses package shipping for all its orders.) The system was then modified to support bulk as well as package shipping, and the new configuration became the new standard.

Using the large and broadly representative implementation team, together with the unit-by-unit rollout, Elf Atochem has been able to staff the effort mainly with its own people. It has had to engage only nine outside consultants to assist in the project—far fewer than is usually the case. The reliance on internal resources not only reduces the cost of the implementation, it also helps ensure that Elf Atochem's employees will understand how the system works after the consultants leave.

Elf Atochem's ES is now more than 75% complete— nine of the 12 business units are up running on the new system—and the rollout is ahead of schedule and under budget. Customer satisfaction levels have already increased, and the company is well on the way to its goal of confirming 95% of all orders with one call, a dramatic improvement over the previous average of five calls. In addition to the service enhancements, the company is operating more efficiently. Inventory levels, receivables, and labor and distribution expenditures have all been cut, and the company expects the system will ultimately reduce annual operating costs by tens of millions of dollars.

The Role of Management

Every company that installs an ES struggles with its cost and complexity. But the companies that have the biggest problems—the kind of problems that can lead to an outright disaster—are those that install an ES without thinking through its full business implications.

Managers may well have good reasons to move fast. They may, for example, have struggled for years with incompatible information systems and may view an ES as a silver bullet. They may be looking for a quick fix to the Year 2000 problem (enterprise systems are not infected with the much-feared millennium bug). Or they may be trying to keep pace with a competitor that has already implemented an ES. The danger is that while an enterprise system may help them meet their immediate challenge, the very act of implementing it may create even larger problems. A speedy implementation of an ES may be a wise business move; a rash implementation is not.

A number of questions should be answered before any decisions are made. How might an ES strengthen our competitive advantages? How might it erode them? What will be the system's effect on our organization and culture? Do we need to extend the system across all our functions, or should we implement only certain modules? Would it be better to roll the system out globally or to restrict it to certain regional units? Are there other alternatives for information management that might actually suit us better than an ES?

A speedy implementation of an enterprise system may be a wise business move, but a rash implementation is not.

The experience of Elf Atochem and other successful adopters of enterprise systems underscores the need for careful deliberation. It also highlights the importance of having top management directly involved in planning and implementing an ES. Not only is Elf Atochem's executive committee overseeing its ES project, but its entire board reviewed and approved the plans. At Compaq, the decision to go with an ES was also made at the board level, and the senior management team was involved with the implementation every step of the way.

Only a general manager is equipped to act as a mediator between the imperatives of the technology and of the business.

Many chief executives, however, continue to view the installation of an ES as primarily a technological challenge. They push responsibility for it down to their information technology departments. Because of an ES's profound business implications—and, in particular, the risk that the technology itself might undermine a company's strategy—off-loading responsibility to technologists is particularly dangerous. Only a general manager is equipped to act as the mediator between the imperatives of the technology and the imperatives of the business. If the development of an enterprise system is not carefully controlled by management, management may soon find itself under the control of the system.

Configuring an Enterprise System

CONFIGURING AN ENTERPRISE SYSTEM is largely a matter of making compromises, of balancing the way you want to work with the way the system lets you work. You begin by deciding which modules to install. Then, for each module, you adjust the system using configuration tables to achieve the best possible fit with your company's processes. Let's look more closely at these two configuration mechanisms:

- **Modules.** Most enterprise systems are modular, enabling a company to implement the system for some functions but not for others. Some modules, such as those for finance and accounting, are adopted by almost all companies that install an ES, whereas others, such as one for human resource management, are adopted by only some companies. Sometimes a company simply doesn't need a module. A service business, for example, is unlikely to require the module for manufacturing. In other cases, companies choose not to implement a module because they already have a serviceable system for that particular function or they have a proprietary system that they believe provides unique benefits. In general, the greater the number of modules selected, the greater the integration benefits, but also the greater the costs, risks, and changes involved.

- **Configuration tables.** A configuration table enables a company to tailor a particular aspect of the system to the way it chooses to do business. An organization can select, for example, what kind of inventory accounting—FIFO or LIFO—it will employ or whether it wants to recognize product revenue by geographical unit, product line, or distribution channel. SAP's R/3, one of the more comprehensive and complex ES offerings, has more than 3,000 configuration tables. Going through all of them can take a long time. Dell Computer, for example, spent more than a year on the task.

  Although modules and configuration tables let you customize the system to some degree, your options will be limited. If you have an idiosyncratic way of doing business, you will likely find that it is not supported by an ES. One company, for example, had long had a practice of giving preferential treatment to its most important customers by occasionally shipping them products that had already been allocated to other accounts. It found that its ES did not allow it the flexibility required to expedite orders in this way. Another company had always kept track of revenues by both product and geography, but its ES would allow it to track revenue in only one way.

  What happens when the options allowed by the system just aren't good enough? A company has two choices, neither of them ideal. It can actually rewrite some of the ES's code, or it can continue to use an existing system and build interfaces between it and the ES. Both of these routes add time and cost to the implementation effort. Moreover, they can dilute the ES's integration benefits. The more customized an enterprise system becomes, the less able it will be to communicate seamlessly with the systems of suppliers and customers.

Originally published in July–August 1998
Reprint 98401

Connectivity and Control in the Year 2000 and Beyond

INTRODUCTION BY RICHARD L. NOLAN

Executive Summary

BY NOW, MOST EXECUTIVES ARE FAMILIAR with the famous Year 2000 problem—and many believe that their companies have the situation well in hand. After all, it seems to be such a trivial problem—computer software that interprets "00" to be the year 1900 instead of the year 2000. And yet armies of computer professionals have been working on it—updating code in payroll systems, distribution systems, actuarial systems, sales-tracking, and the like.

The problem is pervasive. Not only is it in your systems, it's in your suppliers' system's, your bankers' systems, and your customers' systems. It's embedded in chips that control elevators, automated teller machines, process-control equipment, and power grids. Already, a dried-food manufacturer destroyed millions of dollars of perfectly good product when a computer counted inventory marked with an expiration date of "00" as nearly a hundred years old. And when managers of a sewage-control plant turned the clock to January 1, 2000 on a computer system they thought had been fixed, raw sewage pumped directly into the harbor.

It has become apparent that there will not be enough time to find and fix all of the problems by January 1, 2000. And what good will it do if your computers work but they're connected with systems that don't? That is one of the questions Harvard Business School professor Richard Nolan asks in his introduction to HBR's Perspectives on the Year 2000 issue. How will you prepare your organization to respond when things start to go wrong? Fourteen commentators offer their ideas on how senior managers should think about connectivity and control in the year 2000 and beyond.

BY NOW, MOST, IF NOT ALL, SENIOR MANAGERS are well aware of the Year 2000 problem, commonly known as Y2K. But being aware and being in control are not the same. This seemingly trivial situation—the need to correct software programs that understand the impending "00" year code as "1900" instead of "2000"—is turning out to be much harder to address than most people thought, on several levels.

Why? Because the problem is much more pervasive than it appears, and too many companies have failed to recognize that fact for too long. It's one thing to correct code that is readily visible—in payroll systems, for example, or in distribution and sales-tracking programs. But what of the code embedded in the tens of billions of microprocessor chips installed in automated teller machines, elevators, process control equipment, global positioning systems, and the like?

Managers of a sewage-control plant, for instance, thought they had the problem solved when they tested their facility for Year 2000 compliance—that is, tested to see if the plant's systems would work after the turn of the millennium. But when they performed the test by setting the clocks on the plant's computers to January 1, 2000, they were surprised to find that raw sewage pumped directly into the harbor.

Similarly, in 1997, the *Wall Street Journal* reported that a Year 2000 team from the Federal Aviation Administration discovered a date code problem, not in the application software, but in the hardware of one of its computers. The code enabled the huge, water-cooled mainframe computer to switch automatically from one cooling pump to another. If the problem had not been identified and corrected, the pump's switch could have failed, causing the computer to overheat and malfunction.

The FAA operates more than a couple of dozen IBM mainframe computers that are so old neither the original technical documentation nor the people who wrote the software can be found and consulted about making the systems Year 2000 compliant.

Even if your organization *has* dealt comprehensively with its internal problem, one or more of the organizations your company depends on may not have. Companies throughout the world are running in large part far behind U.S. companies in dealing with the Y2K threat. Many are focused on other, seemingly more immediate, issues. Companies in the European Union, for example, are in the midst of converting to a unified currency, which they need to do by the beginning of 1999. Their consideration of Y2K issues—much less any other, as-yet-unidentified problem relating to the connection of their computer systems to any others—is minimal. And probably more than 70% of Japan's CEOs are unaware of the potential of the Y2K problem to disrupt their business and are not providing any meaningful Y2K leadership.

What good does it do you if your computers are Year 2000 compliant but they can't order from your suppliers' computers or ship to your customers' computers? More than 300 million PCs are connected to one another in internal intranets and over the Internet. We have come to depend on them to coordinate supply chains between our companies in real time. Beyond the boundaries of your organization, your ability to identify and correct Y2K errors rapidly diminishes.

To muddle matters even more, a rapidly growing industry of legal counsel and liability insurance has grown up around the Y2K issue. And even as estimates of the cost of fixing the Y2K problem climb to the hundreds of billions of dollars, estimates of the cost of litigation that may be brought against senior managers and boards of directors by shareholders, suppliers, customers, and lenders have risen to a trillion dollars. Such after-the-fact faultfinding will ultimately offer little satisfaction: What good will compensation be if the business has lost its footing and momentum and is critically wounded?

It's true that some companies and industries have made great strides in dealing with the problem and in helping other companies to do so. IBM, for example, has built a Web site (www.yr2k.raleigh.IBM.com) that allows companies to search databases showing the Y2K status of every computer system it has ever built. Large financial-services companies are reputed to have dealt successfully with Y2K on most fronts. And some experts believe that the repercussions of the issue have been vastly overstated. But I don't agree.

Consider just the direct costs of fixing the Y2K problem. I believe that the estimates placing the cost of Y2K compliance conservatively in the tens of millions of dollars for most companies and in the hundreds of millions of dollars for large financial institutions are correct. And keep in mind, those costs produce no revenue. What's more, the Y2K problem has already had a profoundly negative effect on some businesses. Important software projects are being put on hold as large numbers of software engineers and significant amounts of money that might otherwise be directed to revenue-producing investments are being diverted to the task of going through existing software programs to find the deviant Y2K code, fixing it, and then testing it in a newly constructed computer environment that parallels the real one.

Even more disruptive is the economic impact of slowing down the ongoing transformation and consolidation of a number of industries. For example, in the financial services market, the merger-and-acquisition process has led companies to consolidate and close uneconomic bank branches and has produced healthy innovations in products and services. But now, and into the next year, a substantial amount of the key technical resources needed to integrate the computer systems underlying those consolidations will simply be unavailable.

The now-familiar episode in which a supermarket chain's point-of-sale checkout terminals shut down totally when a customer swiped through a bankcard that had an expiration date of 2000 is just the beginning of widespread trouble. Every day, more than 14 million terminals are used to authorize credit cards. Even if cards expiring in the year 2000 are accepted by every one of those systems, trouble can still arise if the terminals are connected to the noncompliant systems of other banks, merchants, or third-party processors. These daily events are further dissipating scarce technical resources as companies scramble to fix newly discovered problems.

I believe that such incidents will multiply, triggering chain reactions that will waste a startling amount of resources. And while such direct costs are huge, I think that the indirect costs are even higher.

Consider an IT department that essentially needs to go back 20 years in time to deal with archaic software that few of its members have been trained in or want to work with. The company has no choice, but mobile software engineers do. Expect already high turnover rates to accelerate—while the clock is ticking. And if regulatory or tax authorities of a particular country become Y2K laggards, international commerce will be swiftly and significantly affected. Component suppliers that show any signs of Y2K-compliance problems will be rapidly replaced by suppliers that don't have the problems.

Information about Y2K problems flows instantly and can be acted on immediately, causing a supplier's revenue to nosedive; unfortunately, fixing the Y2K problems takes much longer. All in all, the Y2K problem stands to have a profoundly negative effect not only on individuals but also on national markets and on economies worldwide.

And make no mistake about it, Y2K is not an isolated problem. Rather, it is the leading example of a class of issues—a new kind of uncertainty brewing as the world becomes more connected electronically—that senior managers are going to face with increasing frequency.

Which is why we have asked 14 individuals, each expert in a different aspect of the Y2K problem, to discuss the issue and offer their ideas on how senior managers should think about connectivity and control in the year 2000 and beyond.

JACK BRENNAN *is the chairman and CEO of the Vanguard Group, based in Valley Forge, Pennsylvania.*

Most senior managers are aware of the Year 2000 problem. And yet, just last month an acquaintance of mine—a director of a company I won't name—asked me about it, thinking it was a celebration of some kind. It's frightening that there are still pockets of ignorance among key constituencies at corporations—especially since each one is another way the Y2K problem could remain untreated, leaving vulnerable even those who are most prepared.

Y2K presents senior managers with a serious problem and an immutable deadline. (If you have not yet begun to address the problem, you are indeed in trouble.) But the issue also presents senior managers with an opportunity to look at the bigger picture. You can—and should—use the Y2K issue as a way to create awareness

Y2K is not a glamorous issue, but it is a major priority; if the best and brightest aren't on the team, you have a problem.

among board members, senior managers, and employees throughout your company of the risks and opportunities afforded by technology.

Ultimately, we all want to make sure we begin the next millennium with vibrant and functioning organizations. And the way to do that is to treat Y2K both as an issue unto itself and as a catalyst spurring us to think about the broader issues associated with our rapidly increasing reliance on technology.

A proper Y2K strategy requires both an offensive and

a defensive posture. The offensive strategy should be focused on what I'll call the *controllables*—the internal technologies and procedures that must be ready for the new millennium. With enough money and time, the obvious technical problems can be solved. But you shouldn't take for granted that they will be. You must be aggressive—or run the risk of finding out when it is too late that you should have been.

Ask two questions. First, have your IT and business organizations put their best people on the project—not simply the people available, but the best people? Y2K is not a glamorous issue, but it is a major priority; if the best and brightest aren't on the team, you have a problem right there. Second, are your various teams fixing each affected system individually and, if so, how are you making sure that those individual changes will function collectively when the time comes? Time may be short, but quick fixes in many different places are not the answer. You need to be certain that all of your systems can—and will—interrelate as they should. These technical challenges seem sort of easy in the grand scheme, but your answers to those two questions will determine whether you are really ready.

Now consider your constituencies: your board, your clients, your employees, and your regulators. Think about how any miscommunication—or lack of communication—could affect the performance of your organization and take steps to ensure that your communication procedures are in place and up to the challenge. It is critical that you keep these constituencies up to date and informed.

Your board, for example, should be given regular progress reports, details of your successes and failures, access to your plans as they evolve, and so on. You should maintain an open dialogue with your clients—

discuss with them the scope of the issue, the program you have in place to fix it, and your contingency plans. Aggressive communication with clients will go a long way toward reducing their stress levels.

Employees at all levels need to be aware of the hard and soft costs of Y2K. They also need to know your priorities: What does the company expect of them, when, and why? How do your Y2K efforts fit into the ongoing business plan? You need to create a sense of accountability in everyone; your employees must be made aware that the Year 2000 problem will not simply go away and have no effect on the bottom line. You must help your employees maintain perspective and, frankly, become watchdogs for potential problem areas. Finally, don't forget about regulators. I realize that financial businesses like mine are somewhat different from those in most industries in the degree to which they are regulated, but an open dialogue with all stakeholders is critical in any case.

Now for the defensive strategy. A good defense will make the difference between those organizations that begin the new millennium with their reputation and operations intact and those that don't.

Consider your interdependencies with other organizations: vendors, clients, utilities—even competitors, in some instances. There will be problems (we don't know where, but think back to my friend and the "celebration"), and they will affect your company. The problems may be as broad as the Internal Revenue Service being unable to collect taxes or as local as a utility company being unable to turn the lights on at your office on January 1, 2000.

We're all participants in financial markets, in government, in electronic connections; somewhere, there will be a problem. The question you have to ask is Am I prepared to deal with any given Y2K-related problem as I would any other contingency that might arise?

I think most organizations should be spending time conducting dry runs and planning for possible scenarios. Call it constructive paranoia, if you will. Look at your normal contingency plans and presume that parts of them will have to be implemented at the beginning of the new millennium. Your entire organization, in fact, should be preparing itself to implement those plans as designed and rehearsed. No doubt various crisis strategies have been written up and filed away. Dust them off and update them for Y2K issues. The hope, of course, is that you won't need them, but prudence says you should be prepared for what may very well happen. Think about risk mitigation and about communication. How will you cordon off any affected areas of your organization so that they have as little negative impact as possible? How will you reintegrate them once the crisis has passed? Who needs to know what and when?

Can any good come out of all this work? Is it all a high-risk, no-reward investment of time, money, and people? I don't think so. Not when you look at the potential results of all the energy that will be spent.

For example, consider the enhanced knowledge you will have about the quality of your IT organization, about its planning and implementation skills, and about your company as a whole. This is a high-stress, high-pressure issue with an immovable deadline—think about what lessons you can learn from the way you handle it.

Consider, also, the intimate knowledge you are being forced to gain about your technical assets and liabilities—whether about the quality and capabilities of your IT organization itself or about the hardware and software your company uses. What computer systems do

vice reps found that they certainly are not ready now. A few companies quoted generic policy statements; the others ranged from making bold statements to not understanding the issues at all. Policies, scripts, and training now could save you lost customers and lawsuits later.

• As the big day approaches, you will want to back up your financial records. Do you intend to request paper copies of key records from your bank on December 31, 1999? Probably—but so will every other company. Log your formal request now. Otherwise, as the millennium approaches, your banking partners will gladly agree to send copies—but not until mid-January 2000, after they have caught up with their backlog of similar, earlier requests.

• Early planning will also be the key to successfully handling the problems that arise on the day itself. For example, suppose that on your factory floor, your process-control and inventory-management systems order the destruction of your products. This has already happened: one dried-food manufacturer destroyed millions of dollars of good product when a computer decided inventory with an expiration date of "00" was nearly a hundred years old. Should your floor supervisors keep or destroy the suspect inventory? Don't be too quick to say they should ignore the "silly" computer order. What if the same program controls the mixture of 12 chemical ingredients? Do you want your supervisors betting that the only error the program made was the destruction order? If you do not want your supervisors to decide, do they know whom to call? Only if you have trained them in advance.

- Forget calling the computer help desk on the day you need it most. That's right, support you count on every day will not be there. It's a simple matter of arithmetic. Help desks generally have one phone line for every several-hundred users. Given that one in six of your fellow companies' systems are not likely to be fully compliant—and the fact that some older versions of popular desktop-software programs are also not fully Y2K compliant—you can count on the line being busy when your employees call. So you had better tell them in advance what else they should do.

In general, throughout your company, you need to think through the potential ramifications and fashion the right mix from three basic strategies: prevention, on-the-spot decision-making, and later recovery. Then put in place the records, training, and other steps necessary to support that mix. And if your company's operation or recovery depends on services that may become scarce, such as overnight shipping or capital, lock up capacity now.

Your arch rival could stumble and be punished by the markets. So could an interesting distributor. Do you have sufficient cash to acquire assets of companies that go bust?

Is the Y2K issue all gloom and doom, nothing but a drain on your profits? No. In fact, for the best companies, the Y2K problem actually represents a real opportunity—but only if you are broadly prepared.

Y2K is a chance to capture new customers if your competitors are less prepared than they should be. For example, if you are really bold and highly confident about your preparations and partners, you might be able to offer customers a premium-priced "safe haven" during this period of uncertainty. Or you could consider exploiting your skills in information technology by introducing new information-based products while your competitors are still focusing on merely fixing the problem. For example, in industries like telecommunications, companies that have thus far only managed to stay even with competitors' technology might be able in mid-1999 to launch state-of-the-art product features and billing systems to move ahead. Your competitors will be too busy fighting with Y2K issues to imitate you.

Do you have sufficient cash to acquire assets of companies that go bust? Some experts claim that as many as 15% of all businesses may face bankruptcy because of Y2K operational difficulties or legal liability. Your arch rival could stumble and be punished by the markets. So could an interesting distributor. Will you have the financing ready to do the deal?

If such bold moves do not fit in with your plans, at least use the turn of the millennium to reduce your pressing IT-talent shortage. As you know, some 20% of programming jobs are unfilled today. But for a very brief time after January 2000, thousands of programmers who are currently employed in Y2K-consulting firms will hit the market. It's a one-time-only recruiting opportunity. But by then, the best programmers will already be gone to the companies that have prepared ahead and recruited them in early 1999.

If you have not thought much about these issues, you are not alone. Most companies have done virtually nothing outside their systems department. But the time to develop your plan is now—while you are still creating your 1999 budget, while you still have the time to think through the challenges and train people, and while you can still seize opportunities.

In January 2000, everyone is going to feel stupid. Some will have overprepared and will regret wasted time and money. Others will be in crisis and wish they had focused sooner. But given a choice—and you have one now—we know which of those we'd rather be.

> **NORMAN STRAUSS** *is the national director of accounting standards and* **THOMAS MILAN** *is the director of accounting and professional matters at Ernst & Young in New York.*

The accounting requirements for Y2K costs are clear. We hope that most, if not all, of you know to expense them as they occur. What's not as clear are matters of disclosure. Indeed, companies have only recently begun making disclosures about Y2K and its associated risks in their annual reports to shareholders. We believe that all companies should follow suit. It's good business practice, and it will serve you well in both the short and long terms.

To be sure, some organizations have little choice. The Securities and Exchange Commission expects public companies to disclose material information about operations and liquidity issues in the management discussion and analysis (MD&A) sections of their annual reports. And an informal survey we conducted of calendar 1997 annual reports filed by

Deciding what to disclose and when can help senior managers create a map of the situation for themselves.

publicly held companies showed that most discussed their Y2K issues. That was a great contrast to a similar survey we conducted in 1996, when we found only 6% had made such disclosures.

But even those companies not required to do so should seriously consider sharing information about their Y2K risk-and-mitigation plans with interested constituencies. Such disclosure will reduce uncertainty among stakeholders. An early alert as to the nature and status of the company's Year 2000 problem will go a long way toward mitigating potentially damaging rumors and uninformed reactions. What's more, developing and making disclosures will help senior managers focus attention on the issue, on its potential for damage, and on creating and implementing a plan for its timely resolution. (SEC guidelines for such disclosures can be found in *Staff Legal Bulletin*, Number 5.)

In other words, deciding what Y2K-related issues to disclose and when can help senior managers create a map of the situation for themselves. We recommend the following structure for organizing the relevant information. Even if you are not preparing such a report, the structure may be useful as a diagnostic tool for organizing your approach to the problem:

- Consider first the scope and potential impact of the Y2K problem. What is the nature and extent of the problem as it relates to your company? What is its potential impact on business operations—including operating systems and equipment (cash registers, robotics, and so on)? To what extent is the company vulnerable to the failure of any third parties—such as vendors and major customers—to correct their own problems relating to interface issues? What might

happen if you can't make your products work because
of a Y2K problem?

- Once the nature of the problem has been addressed,
turn to the solution. What do you plan to do? How
much time do you estimate it will take to implement
the various solutions? What's your best estimate of
the cost of the solutions? Will that cost have a material effect on the company's financial results? How do
you plan to address the failures of third parties? How
far along are you in implementing a solution? What
are your expenditures to date?

- Finally, address the unknowns. What are the risks
and uncertainties that might prevent your Year 2000
plans from being successful? Do you have contingency plans for those situations? How will you continue operations in the event that your remediation
plan is faulty?

The SEC guidelines recommend that managers disclose material uncertainties surrounding the effect of
the Y2K problem on their organizations. That is, the
SEC recommends that managers disclose information
about the Y2K issue and their company's plans to deal
with it regardless of how far along they are in implementing solutions. Even if you are way behind the curve
in addressing the problem, pinpointing your where-
abouts will at least give you an idea of the work ahead.
And if you have the problem well in hand, your stakeholders still should be made aware of any potential
effect on the company's business, on its operations, or
on its financial condition, as well as on your plans to
prevent or assuage any damage.

We recommend that disclosures be made on a quarterly basis (although, clearly, there is no need to redisclose information that has not changed). Taking the pulse of the situation on a regular basis is a good idea. Careful, consistent monitoring will help you control what you can of a problem that may have uncontrollable elements.

DEBRA SPEIGHT *is the chief information officer and vice president of information technology at Harvard Pilgrim Health Care in Lexington, Massachusetts.*

What is Y2K really about? Or, rather, from a senior management perspective, what should it be about? First and foremost, it should be about companywide risk mitigation and contingency planning. Senior managers need to recognize that the Y2K problem can and may affect every aspect of their businesses, and they need to treat it with the seriousness that they would any crisis of that scope. That means taking a companywide approach to a solution, not simply relegating the problem to the IT help desk.

Consider the economic impact of providing a manual stopgap solution to a simple glitch in distribution software, even for a short time.

Specifically, it means identifying every possible internal glitch and fixing each so that all systems will continue to work together after the deadline date. It also means identifying—as much as possible—the potential glitches in the systems of vendors, customers, and any partners the business has. It means managing integration testing—internally and externally—as a top business priority. It means planning what to do if the systems fail anyway, at any link in the chain. And it means sticking to a strict due-diligence procedure—however distasteful—with any business partners that do not comply.

Failing to recognize the potential impact of the Y2K problem—and failing to have a contingency plan—will make the inevitable damage even worse. For example, consider the economic impact of providing a manual solution to a glitch in distribution software, even for a short time. If a company can't handle the expense of having people track orders with pen and paper while the automated system is being repaired, the losses incurred will drop straight to the bottom line. Multiply that possibility by however many companies have similar problems, and by the number of other organizations affected by that glitch, and you have a widespread economic disaster.

The Y2K problem is also one of communication. To date, few companies are working together as consortiums to spread awareness of Y2K issues and to put pressure on vendors and other critical organizations to fix the problem. Health care providers, for example, should come together to influence noncompliant pharmaceutical companies. Any company's inattention to this issue could be fatal—to itself and to any other organization that is dependent on it. We need such consortiums in every industry to advocate and to encourage—to force, if necessary—compliance.

Another communication issue is the public's view of the problem. Many consumers reading about the Y2K issue in the press believe that naysayers like myself are vastly overestimating the scope of the problem. As senior managers who are aware of the potential dangers

of the Y2K problem, we have failed thus far to communicate our knowledge effectively to the public, both
directly and through the media. The problem is complex and pervasive, and if we are unable to reverse the
general mind-set that the problem is being overblown,
a good many individuals are going to be blindsided—
potentially making the problem worse when they discover that it's real after all.

Finally, Y2K is going to challenge what we currently
acknowledge to be best practices. Companies that we
now recognize as being particularly good at managing
alliances, for example, will truly be put to the test. The
more integrated businesses are around the globe, the
more at risk they are of a Y2K-related breakdown in
their operations. And what was once a strength may
now become a weakness. Only those that emerge relatively unscathed will still be able to hold up the "best
practice" banner with integrity.

RICHARD S. TEDLOW *is the Class of 1957 Professor of
Business Administration at the Harvard Business School
in Boston, Massachusetts.*

When you look to the future, what are you willing to say
is *inevitable?* You would not want to use that word with
regard to business, the global economy, health care, pop-
ulation, climate, war, or peace. But what would you want
to say is inevitable? What would any five-year-old child
say is inevitable? What would every single individual of
no matter what level of intelligence agree was inevitable?

Everyone would agree that the year following 1999
will be 2000.

Is this news? Did people know this in, say, 1980?
1950? 1900? 1000? 100? Yes, people did know it. Everybody knew it. No, it is not news.

That truth poses an interesting dilemma. How many trillions of dollars have been spent on computers in the past halfcentury? How many of the world's most brilliant minds have worked in the computer industry? How is it possible that all those folks with all those funds only recently discovered what every five-year-old has known for almost two millennia? Which genius was it who figured out that the last two digits of a year were all a computer needed to recognize?

This problem—a completely unintended consequence of technological change—ought to have a name attached to it. It is the last word in Murphy's Law. Contact www.murphy@aol.com.

The fact of the matter is, it is a common occurrence for technological change to produce unintended consequences. Let's take an example from the history of communications. In ancient Egypt, information was first recorded solely on stone. Then someone came up with papyrus. Light and portable, papyrus could easily be transported from place to place, thus transmitting the commands of the monarch to an ever widening territory.

However, papyrus was also scarce, and literacy was rare. Therefore, a special elite class was created to communicate through its use. The monarch's power depended upon them. This is how papyrus contributed to the rise of bureaucracy.[1]

Another intriguing example of the unintended consequences of technological change is the stirrup. How could such a simple device make such a big difference?

Before the stirrup, the horseman sat precariously on his mount. He was, in the words of historian Lynn White, Jr., "primarily a rapidly mobile bowman and hurler of javelins." The stirrup was a revolutionary way for the horseman to brace himself. By providing lateral support, it

> *welded horse and rider into a single fighting unit capable of a violence without precedent. . . .[It] thus replaced human energy with animal power and immensely increased the warrior's ability to damage his enemy. Immediately, without preparatory steps, it made possible mounted shock combat. . . .*

No wonder the stirrup was front-page news when its significance dawned on western Europeans in the eighth century. The horse had become a weapon that would determine the future. But horses are expensive. They require land and fodder. Rulers seized the land available from the church and distributed it to vassals who pledged service in the army when called upon.

This is how the stirrup contributed to the rise of feudalism.[2]

No one woke up one fine day and said, "What we need is bureaucracy; let's have papyrus" or "What we need is feudalism; let's invent the stirrup." The difference between these two unintended consequences and the Year 2000 problem is that they were not only unforeseen, but also unforeseeable. The mystery of the Year 2000 problem is why no one thought about it until so late in the day. One can only hope that the myrmidons of global computing will get us out of this mess.

What's next? That is the real question. Surely if a mistake this basic could be made, others—many others—must be lurking just around the corner.

But what next? That is the real question. Surely if a mistake this basic could be made, others—many others—must be lurking just around the corner. Each will prove to be another chapter in the ongoing saga of the failure of the computer to match its performance to its promise.

DEBORAH GILLOTTI *is the chief information officer of Starbucks Coffee Company in Seattle, Washington.*

Most people think of the Year 2000 issue primarily as an information systems problem. There's no question that computer systems represent a major portion of the overall exposure for most organizations. However, what's easy to overlook is the breadth of potential risk that Y2K problems pose for functions outside the IS domain. Those companies that make remediation a strategic, enterprise initiative—one that the entire senior-management team feels responsible for—will probably be the most successful in mitigating this risk.

Ideally, this remediation should be championed by the CEO, the CFO, or the COO to make sure that it receives the priority it deserves. A tall order? Yes, without a doubt. But consider the impact of any one of many potential disruptions that can occur outside IS, including interactions with trading partners on a global basis. How many organizations can say today that they have an active program to inventory these risks and put specific tactics in place to address them? Are all leaders of business units accountable, as part of their overall objectives, for managing Y2K risks in their own areas?

The reality probably is that, in many cases, this topic has not become a high enough priority for most senior executives because it is considered to be just an IS problem. That is a serious mistake. Y2K is a symbol of how much senior managers may not realize—and need to learn quickly—about the way their businesses operate today. Simply said, it's what you don't know that can really hurt you.

CIOs could play a major role in helping their organizations reduce the potential risk in several ways. First, because their overall understanding of companywide business processes tends to be broader than that of most executives, CIOs are well qualified to lead an enterprisewide remediation effort. They can educate and influence their peers within the organization about the importance of the Y2K issue—and help them start assessing their Y2K risks. Second, the discipline and processes developed to catalog the risks within IS applications can be applied to non-IS business processes, equipment, and the like. Finally, and most important, CIOs can help build awareness about Y2K issues by deploying kiosks, intranet sites, and other technologies for delivering information to employees.

From HVAC systems to the smallest vendor transaction, we need to be more aware of how our organizations are tied inextricably to other constituencies.

In short, the Y2K issue is an opportunity for CIOs to demonstrate the value of their role as a resource with a knowledge base that spans many disciplines and geographic regions. They can ensure that employees at every level are knowledgeable, and accountable, for mitigating Y2K risks. Ideally, the entire organization, not just IS, will feel responsible for finding solutions to the Year 2000 problem.

The Y2K issue has highlighted the need for managers to have a broader and deeper understanding of their business. From HVAC systems to the smallest vendor transaction, we need to be more aware of how our organizations are tied inextricably to other constituencies. We need to better understand the channels of any given transaction or process—who is involved, how reliable each connection is, and how we will respond if any of these connections proves to be faulty.

The Y2K problem has highlighted the need for senior business executives to acquire the more rigorous process orientation that typically has been associated with the IS function. If that mind-set prevails, our companies will move into the next millennium in positions of strength.

DR. EDWARD YARDENI *is the chief economist and a managing director at Deutsche Bank Securities, based in New York.*

Like Captain James T. Kirk in *Star Trek,* most executives know how to fly their enterprises at Warp I. That is, most are comfortable leading their organizations even in today's increasingly wired world of just-in-time manufacturing, outsourcing, and globalization. They are in command and solidly in control. Soon, however, they will have to learn to manage in an entirely different environment—in a world of potentially widespread economic failure. Their enterprises are about to enter Warp II—an unprecedented condition, be it a speed, a space, or a place—as the global computer system goes haywire in the year 2000. Too many top managers remain sadly unaware of that fact, but I believe it to be true. Business leaders are about to lose control. They must, however, continue to lead.

It is time to prepare for failure. The sooner our business and political leaders start to face that concept, the sooner we—as a world of interdependent, interconnected organizations—can begin to rebuild and recover from the coming crash. It's now July 1998. There is not enough awareness, time, and resources to fix every computer system. Most systems will be fixed in time—no doubt, many readers are thinking "*my* organization has this thing well in hand"—but some vitally important ones simply will *not* be ready. In a domino fashion, those systems are bound to disrupt, corrupt, or crash other, compliant systems.

In Warp II, even if an organization fixes all of its IT systems and embedded chips so that they recognize "00" as 2000 and not 1900, those systems can be instantly and severely impaired by bad data coming from external sources. There can be no assurances that even systems that have been fixed will work properly until they are stress tested under Warp II conditions. In the year 2000, executives will not have the luxury of complete confidence in their systems or in those of

A disruption in oil supply caused a global recession in the 1970s; this time the cause will be a disruption in the flow of information.

their utility providers, shippers, vendors, customers, or creditors. Expecting a flawless transition, then, would be unreasonable; such blind confidence would be foolhardy. So CEOs must prepare now to fly as best they can in a suddenly alien global economy. They must begin to ask themselves what-if kinds of questions and to think through some plausible solutions to the problems those questions raise.

What if their electric utility providers are not ready for the date change? What if their fuel supplies and transportation lines are not secure? What if the phone system goes down? What if the phones work but become overloaded? What if the Federal Aviation Administration's noncompliant and aging computers are not replaced in time to support the current load of air traffic?

What if your bank won't roll over your loan in 1999, concluding that there is a risk your systems won't be ready for the year 2000? What if some of your key vendors, distributors, and customers face a Y2K-related credit crunch next year? Should you lend them money or acquire them? How quickly can you fold their noncompliant IT systems into your compliant ones?

Even if an organization and its entire supply, distribution, and customer chain remain intact and completely functional in 2000, a global recession is likely. It could be as bad as or worse than the 1973–1974 global recession. A severe disruption in the supply of oil depressed global business back then; today, it will be a disruption in the flow of information. Even worse is the likelihood that the information that does continue to flow could be corrupt. Imagine what would have happened if gasoline that had been mixed with water were unknowingly pumped into gas tanks as motorists desperately sought to fill their tanks during the oil crisis.

I could be wrong about my grim scenario for the year 2000. I hope I am. But the foremost question right now must be Are our business leaders prepared to command if I am right? We will need all the leadership skills of our executives to maneuver us out of the dangerous Warp II, back to the safer Warp I. Now is the time to form industry alliances to minimize the potential disruptions and to prepare quick responses to unexpected breaks in the chain. Now is the time to identify the weak links in our just-in-time world and to build just-in-case buffers. Now is the time to put maximum pressure on those who are not taking the Y2K issue seriously enough.

And now is the time to alert the public. Business and government leaders must communicate as never before, lest their constituents panic when things begin to go wrong. Some people, for example, are already talking about taking their money out of the bank and the stock market in mid-1999 and keeping it as cash. Imagine several possible outcomes to the Y2K crisis, ranging in severity from minor disruptions to meltdown. Business and government leaders can have a great hand in which of those comes to pass. It's up to top managers in both spheres to say, "This is what might happen. This is how we're preparing for it. Don't panic."

Take banking, for instance. Top managers must prepare the public for the possibility that ATMs won't work or will be unreliable in reporting balances and transactions. Managers must explain to their customers what might happen and how they have planned to solve the problem. They must reassure their clients that they have hard copies of the pertinent information and that the problem will be fixed within a specified time. Without such leadership, panic is likely—and panic will only lead to further disruption. With leadership, we'll all get through this on a faster, less bumpy course.

Ultimately, of course, business leaders should begin to think of Y2K as a huge—albeit painful—wake-up call. The fact is that in the coming millennium, executives will have to be as conversant with technology as they are today with finance, marketing, and other areas of management. IT must become one of those disciplines that all senior executives know backwards and forwards— not just how to use the information IT can provide, but how that information is procured, where the connections are made, and what electronic interdependencies exist within their own organizations and between themselves and others.

The Y2K crisis is occurring because top managers have neglected IT. A vitally important function was not given the recognition and attention it deserved. That must change—Y2K will force that change. And in doing so, it will force a better understanding of the drivers of business into the future.

DENNIS J. BLOCK *and* **STEPHEN A. RADIN** *are members of the law firm Weil, Gotshal & Manges in New York.*

Shareholder litigation against the directors and officers of corporations that experience Year 2000 problems is almost a certainty. That's why it's a good idea to know about the two forms of litigation against directors and officers that we believe will be the most prevalent. Understanding where you may be vulnerable may help you craft and implement strategies now to protect yourself.

The first type of litigation will be *shareholder derivative suits* alleging that directors breached their fiduciary duty of care to the corporation by failing to properly oversee the corporation's business. These suits will seek to recover whatever losses the corporation experiences as a result of the Year 2000 problem.

The defense against such a suit is relatively straightforward. If board members have heard reports and recommendations from their employees or from consultants, and based on those reports and recommendations they determine that their corporation's computer systems (and the systems of its suppliers and relevant customers) are appropriately equipped to deal with the Year 2000 problem, that decision—however wrong it may ultimately prove to be—will be protected by the *business judgment rule.* The rule holds that board members are required to do no more than make an "informed effort" to serve the best interests of shareholders.

If, however, board members have not made *any* decisions concerning their company's Y2K problems or have made decisions without seeking appropriate input, they may have a more difficult time winning a shareholder suit alleging a breach of fiduciary duty. When shareholders allege that directors are to blame for corporate problems due to oversight failures, courts typically look to see whether the directors were "on notice" of the potential problem. That is, they look to see if directors were made aware of the potential problem, had adequate information about the potential consequences, and had adequate time to act. Courts typically have not found a sufficient basis on which to assess directors' liability in such cases, but Y2K-related cases could set a precedent. The countless articles on Y2K that have appeared in the media arguably put directors in almost every corporation on notice of the issue in a way that would require their action.

Even in such a case, however, directors who do not act in accordance with their duty of care still are likely to be protected from liability. Most states have enacted statutes—sometimes referred to as raincoat statutes—that allow shareholders to adopt provisions in their corporate charter that preclude personal liability for violations of the directors' duty. And the shareholders of many corporations have adopted such charter provisions.

> *Directors should keep a record of what is being done at the board level to protect themselves.*

A second form of litigation will be class actions brought by shareholders against the corporation, directors, and officers. These suits will seek to recover whatever losses the shareholders experience as a result of any

drop in stock price caused by Y2K problems. A shareholder might point to statements by a corporation
concerning the Year 2000 issue (for example, that the
corporation's computer systems were properly equipped
to deal with Year 2000 issues) and allege that those
statements were false or misleading. A shareholder
also might point to the corporation's failure to disclose
that its most important supplier or customer was ill-
equipped to do business in the year 2000 and that, as a
result, the corporation's business would be adversely
affected. If the corporation did not communicate with
shareholders at all about the issue, those shareholders
might contend that it was false and misleading not to
have been told that the corporation, its suppliers, and its
customers faced Y2K problems. Suits of this type will
allege that statements (or omissions) in the corporation's disclosure documents caused investors to buy
stock at inflated prices or to elect directors thinking that
those directors would take appropriate action to deal
with Y2K issues when, in fact, they did not.

Directors, officers, and corporate counsel need to
focus on Y2K issues now—both to avoid or minimize
potential problems and related losses for their corporations and to protect themselves from personal liability if
Y2K problems do result in losses to the corporation and
its shareholders. Directors serving on boards that have
not yet discussed Y2K should raise the issue now. They
should also create and keep a record of what is being
done at the board level to protect themselves if they do
face litigation in the year 2000 and beyond. Directors also
should make certain that the corporation does not agree
to exclusions that might restrict coverage for Y2K claims
in any directors-and-officers (D&O) insurance policies
purchased or renewed between now and the year 2000.

Finally, now is the time to provide material information to investors and to make certain that all reporting obligations required by the Securities and Exchange Commission have been met. Doing so is required by law and will allow corporations to minimize the possibility that shareholders can claim the corporation's disclosures were false or misleading or that directors were elected improperly because investors were not told the truth about Y2K.

STEVE SHEINHEIT *is the director of corporate systems and architecture with enterprisewide Year 2000 responsibility at the Chase Manhattan Bank.* BRIAN ROBBINS *leads Chase's Year 2000 Enterprise Program. Both are based in New York.*

It doesn't matter how much you've accomplished with regard to preparations for the year 2000, you've probably still got a long way to go.

At Chase, we've been working on the issue in an organized fashion since 1995. Even though we have accomplished much since then—upgrading the systems used to book loans and calculate investment returns beyond the turn of the century, for example—Y2K still represents a very large-scale systems- and business-integration effort for us.

To tackle it, we've established 30 project offices to handle nearly 300 individual projects covering approximately 3,000 business applications. As many as 1,500 people will work on the problem this year, and nearly $300 million will be spent between January 1997 and December 1999. Make no mistake, however. No matter how good a handle you have on your Year 2000 preparations, the fact is related problems are pervasive and devilishly difficult to track and fix completely.

To say, with confidence, that your organization has the Y2K issue under control, Y2K must be a top priority, after day-to-day production, throughout the company.

For example, you have to know how and how fast the technical issues are being addressed. Testing represents the bulk of the work and automated test tools can help, but there is no panacea. Highly skilled and knowledge-able systems and business professionals are the essential ingredients in building the complex set of test scripts that will be required for your systems testing.

You also need to track the management of the issue—both internally and externally. And for that, you must not rely solely on status reports—hands-on monitoring by senior managers will be necessary.

Expect problems to occur before January 1, 2000, and for some time thereafter, despite your best efforts. Examples of Y2K problems have already surfaced. Credit cards with year 2000 expiration dates have been rejected by some point-of-sale terminals. One food manufacturer destroyed a perfectly good batch of product because it thought the freshness date had passed.

At Chase, we've occasionally encountered unexpected snafus. For example, on January 1, 1998, our application for maintaining stop-payment orders on checks treated all of that day's stop payments as "expired." What happened? Chase normally holds stop payments for two years, but due to a computer-system Y2K date-logic error, these expired in one day instead. The point is, no matter how well prepared you are, and at Chase we feel we have the Y2K problem well in hand, moderate business disruptions are likely to occur. Only proper planning can prevent these from escalating into major problems.

You should also be clear about the risks your business faces if your system—or any your organization depends on—fails. Keep in mind, what you do in the face of problems now and how you react to your customers' and business partners' problems can make the difference between a business loss and an opportunity to build a relationship.

Know that you are not alonè in worrying about the "other guy." The level of interdependency among organizations is probably the most vexing issue for professionals involved in Y2K. Due diligence processes for reviewing business relationships and assessing new opportunities should take into account Y2K risks. At Chase, that process has included enhancing our credit-review and risk-rating procedures. You must extend your thinking to your company's entire supply chain. For financial institutions, for example, that chain could include funds providers, subcustodians, correspondent banks, and the major clearing organizations that make up the global settlement system. Contingency planning is a must—don't hesitate to establish backup vendors and suppliers and to use them if your current business partners have problems.

Realize, too, that Y2K does offer some business opportunities. You can, potentially, use the Y2K issue as an opportunity to strengthen your information technology portfolio, lowering the risk of long-term effects and, at the same time, establishing a competitive advantage.

While it would be ideal to leverage your investment dollars by aligning Y2K projects with the reengineering of business practices, it's probably too late to do so. Wherever possible, however, you should use your Y2K activities as a way to enhance your post-2000 technology environment. For example, the testing and quality assurance disciplines you put in place for Y2K can be incorporated into future business processes.

Finally, don't underestimate the importance of proactive, consistent communication in enhancing value. If your program is solid, and you communicate openly and clearly with all your stakeholders, you will build goodwill and trust that should serve as a foundation to carry you well into the next century.

Notes

1. This story is told in Erik Barnouw, *A Tower in Babel: A History of Broadcasting in the United States to 1933* (New York: Oxford University Press, 1966), p. 3.

2. The classic account is Lynn White, Jr., *Medieval Technology and Social Change* (London: Oxford University Press, 1962), pp. 1–38.

Originally published in July–August 1998
Reprint 98411

About the Contributors

GENE BATCHELDER is the senior vice president, treasurer, controller, and chief financial officer of GPM Gas Corporation and of Phillips Gas Company, the Houston-based subsidiary of Phillips Petroleum Company. He was named to his current position in 1994. Previously, he was president of Phillips Driscopipe, Inc., also a subsidiary of Phillips Petroleum Company.

JOHN CROSS is the CIO of the British Petroleum Company (BP) and is responsible for integrating the separate IT activities in the firm's business streams. An economist at Shell, he joined BP in 1976 when a joint Shell-BP operating company was divided. During the 1980s, Mr. Cross was responsible for human resource policy development, with a focus on white collar unions and compensation policy.

THOMAS H. DAVENPORT is the director of the Institute for Strategic Change at Andersen Consulting. Previously he was a professor of information management at the University of Texas, Austin, and a director of research at Ernst & Young, McKinsey & Company, and CSC Index. Mr. Davenport is the author of *Process Innovation* (HBS Press, 1993) and the co-author, with Laurence Prusak, of *Working Knowledge: How Organizations Manage What They Know* (HBS Press, 1998).

DAVID F. FEENY is vice president of Templeton College, Oxford, and director of the Oxford Institute of Information Management. His interests center on the connections among strategy, organization, and information management. His focus includes the role of IT in creating strategic advantage, the implementation of major IT-based projects, and the sourcing of IT services. Mr. Feeny's recent research has been about creating organizational arrangements that foster strategic exploitation of IT. His work has won international recognition and has been published in the leading IS and general management journals, including the *Harvard Business Review,* the *Sloan Management Review,* and the *McKinsey Quarterly.*

JEROME H. GROSSMAN, M.D., is the chairman and CEO of Health Quality, Inc., dedicated to developing measurement and information solutions for providers and purchasers of health care. He is also chairman emeritus of New England Medical Center, Inc. Recognized as an expert and a proponent of outcomes and health services research as a means of improving health, Dr. Grossman founded The Health Institute at New England Medical Center in 1988 for the purpose of expanding the Medical Center's research capacity to include the social sciences as well as the natural sciences. Dr. Grossman has been a member of the founding team of several health care companies.

STEPHAN H. HAECKEL is director of Strategic Studies at IBM's Advanced Business Institute, where he conducts research, teaches, and advises clients on the use of information and technology to design and implement adaptive enterprises. His current research interests include the issues associated with managing in information-rich environments, and the extension of customer value propositions to incorporate experiential values. Mr. Haeckel is chairman of the Marketing

Science Institute and represents IBM in the Marketing Council of the American Management Association.

RICHARD L. HUBER is the president and chief executive officer of Aetna, Inc. A director since September 1996, he joined the company as vice chairman in February 1995, and he retained his role as the company's vice chairman and chief financial officer until he was elected chairman in 1997. Immediately before joining Aetna, Mr. Huber was president and chief operating officer of Grupo Wasserstein Perella, where he was responsible for developing the investment and merchant banking activities throughout Latin America for Wasserstein Perella, a leading investment banking firm.

MARY C. LACITY is an associate professor of MIS at the University of Missouri–St. Louis and a research affiliate at Templeton College, Oxford University. Her research focuses on IT management practices in the areas of sourcing, IT privatization, benchmarking, IT metrics, and client/server development. She is the coauthor, with Rudy Hirschheim, of *Information Systems Outsourcing: Myths, Metaphors, and Realities* and *Beyond the Information Systems Outsourcing Bandwagon: The Insourcing Response* and the coeditor, with Leslie Willcocks, of *Strategic Sourcing of Information Systems.* Her articles have appeared in such journals as the *Harvard Business Review* and the *Sloan Management Review.*

BOB L. MARTIN is the president and chief executive officer of Wal-Mart International. He remains an executive vice president of Wal-Mart Stores, Inc., as well as a member of Wal-Mart's executive committee. Mr. Martin is the chief executive responsible for the development and operation of the company's interest outside the United States. The operating division is comprised of Wal-Mart's Discount Stores, Wal-Mart Supercenters, and its Sam's Wholesale Club concepts, currently operating in eight countries.

JONATHAN NEWCOMB is the president and chief executive officer of Simon & Schuster, the world's largest educational, computer, and English-language book publisher. During his tenure as CEO, Mr. Newcomb has redefined Simon & Schuster as a full-line, technology-based, multiple-media global publisher and has become one of the world's most prolific interactive publishers.

RICHARD L. NOLAN is the William Barclay Harding Professor of Management of Technology at Harvard Business School. Professor Nolan returned to the faculty of Harvard Business School in 1991, after serving as chairman of Nolan, Norton & Co. since 1977. He is currently studying business transformation, the process of creatively destroying industrial economy management principles and evolving workable management principles for the information economy. He is co-author, with David Croson, of *Creative Destruction: A Six-Stage Process for Transforming the Organization* (HBS Press, 1995) and, with Thomas Davenport, Donna L. Stoddard, and Sirkka Jarvenpaa, *Reengineering the Organization,* (Harvard Business School Publishing, 1995). His latest book, edited with Stephen P. Bradley, is *Sense and Respond: Capturing Value in the Network Era* (HBS Press, 1998).

JOHN F. ROCKART is the director of the center for Information Systems Research and a senior lecturer at the Sloan School of Management, MIT. He is best known for the development of the critical success factors (CSF) method for information and information systems planning and for the seminal articles that initiated the field of executive support systems (ESS). His current research interests include the extension of ESS concepts into management support systems, new software methods and tools for more effective systems development, and the future of the IT organization. He is the coeditor, with Christine V. Bullen, of *The Rise of Managerial Computing* and the coauthor, with Michael S. Scott Morton, of *Computers and the Learning Process* and, with David W. De Long, of *Executive Support Systems: The Emergence of Top Management Computer Use.*

LESLIE P. WILLCOCKS is a fellow at the Oxford Institute of Information Management at Templeton College. Renowned for his work on information management, evaluation, and IT outsourcing, he is a frequent keynote speaker at practitioner and academic conferences throughout the world. Mr. Willcocks is the coauthor of 14 books, the most recently of which is *New Strategies in IT Outsourcing.* He is also the editor-in-chief of the *Journal of Information Technology.*

WAYNE P. YETTER is the president and chief executive officer of Novartis Pharmaceuticals Corporation. Prior to assuming leadership of Novartis Pharmaceuticals, he was president and chief executive officer of Astra Merck Inc. He was named to this position in November 1994, when the company—formerly a unit of Merck & Company, Inc.—became a freestanding joint venture owned equally by Merck and Astra AB of Sweden.

Index

accountability
    enterprise systems modeling
        and, 145
    line managers and, 45
accounting, and Y2K problem,
    202–205
Air Products and Chemicals,
    170–171
Alyeska Pipeline Services
    Company, 102
American Airlines, 10
    SABRE reservation system,
        36
Andersen Consulting, 59, 123,
    124
annual reports, and Y2K prob-
    lem, 202–205
antitrust law, European, 95
Apple Computer, 169
Applied Materials, 161
Astra Merck, 36, 50–54
Autodesk, 167
automated processes. *See*
    enterprise systems; pro-
    cess control

banking industry, and Y2K
    problem, 214, 215
Batchelder, Gene, 36, 40–43
benchmarking, 98
best practices, and Y2K prob-
    lem, 207
Block, Dennis J., 216–219
board of directors, and Y2K
    problem, 194–195,
    216–219
BP Exploration. *See* British
    Petroleum Company
Bramley, John, 92
Brennan, Jack, 193–197
British Petroleum Company,
    83–105
    assessment of potential IT
        suppliers at, 93–99
    outsourcing challenges at,
        99–105
    selective outsourcing
        approach and, 87–93
British Telecommunications.
    See Syncordia
Britoil, 87

Brooklyn Union Gas of New
York, 138–141, 143, 156
BSP. *See* "business systems
planning"
business documents, 25–26
*A Business Guide to Outsourc-
ing* (Willcocks and
Fitzgerald), 75
Business Integration Council
(GPM Gas Corporation),
42
business judgment rule, 216
"business systems planning"
(BSP), 6
business units, coordination of,
155. *See also* enterprise
systems

Center for Information Systems Research (MIT),
47–50
Chase Manhattan Bank, 219
Chemical Bank, 14–16
chief executive officer (CEO).
See also manage-by-wire
system
enterprise systems and, 144,
181–183
investment decisions and,
35–56
outsourcing and, 61–62, 81
chief financial officer (CFO),
62, 63
chief information officer (CIO)
IT effectiveness and, 49–50
management role of, 36,

39–40, 43, 45, 46
outsourcing and, 62, 123
Y2K problem and, 197, 211
Citibank, 114
class action suits, 217–218
clients, and Y2K problem,
194–195
commodity systems, and IT
outsourcing, 58–59,
62–65, 73
communication
alternatives for, 19–20
IT investment emphasis on,
39
outsourcing decisions and,
128–129
Y2K problem and, 194–195,
202–205, 206–207, 219,
222
Compaq Computer, 169–170,
182
competitive advantage
enterprise systems and,
169–171, 179
IT investment decisions
and, 48–49, 54–56
IT outsourcing and, 59, 66,
115–116, 121
computer help desks, and Y2K
problem, 200
Computer Sciences Corporation, 59, 123
Computer Task Group (CTG),
102
configuration tables, in enterprise systems, 184

connecting, and corporate IQ,
142, 153
constituencies, and Y2K problem, 194–195
constructive paranoia, 196
consultants
internal IT consulting and,
103–105
outsourcing decisions and,
129
Y2K opportunities and, 201
Continental Bank, 107–129
challenges to recovery and,
110–113
choice of outsourcing suppliers and, 120–125
implementation of IT out-
sourcing at, 117–120
IT outsourcing decision at,
113–117
liquidity crisis at, 108–110
results of outsourcing decision at, 125–128
contingency planning, and
Y2K, 196, 205–207
contract-management teams,
78–79
control
IT outsourcing decision
and, 59, 88–89
Y2K problem and, 212
controllables, and Y2K,
194–195
core competencies, and IT outsourcing, 114–115
corporate culture

enterprise systems and, 172
outsourcing and, 112
corporate IQ, 141–142
assessment of, 152–154
enterprise systems and,
145–151
costs
BP's outsourcing strategy
and, 89–90, 92, 100
enterprise system imple-
mentation and, 170–171
of fragmented information
systems, 164–165
outsourcing at Continental
Bank and, 109, 116
Y2K problem and, 190–191,
202–205
Coyne, Kevin P., 197–202
CRIS. *See* Customer-Related
Information System
CTG. *See* Computer Task
Group
Customer-Related Information
System (CRIS), 139–141,
143
customer service, and Y2K
problem, 198–199

data models, 149–150. *See also*
enterprise systems
Dean Witter, 26
decision making, 6, 7. *See also*
information technology
investments
delivery systems, 49
Dell Computer, 161

Deutsche Bank Securities,
212–216
Digital Equipment Corporation, 9
TeamLinks groupware, 26
directors-and-officers (D&O)
insurance policies, 218
disclosure, and Y2K problem,
202–205, 218, 219
discount retail industry. *See*
Wal-Mart Stores
D&O policies. *See* directors-
and-officers insurance
policies
Dow Chemical, 161–162, 173
Drucker, Peter F., 47

Eastman Kodak, 59
economic issues, and Y2K,
191–192, 206, 214
EDS, 59
EDS-Scicon, 87
efficiency, and IT outsourcing,
73–74
Elf Atochem North America,
176–181, 182
e-mail
junk mail problem and,
17–18
relationships and, 18–19
employees
IT outsourcing and,
117–118, 122–123,
126–127
Y2K problem and, 195, 198,
199
Energen (fictitious company)

choice of suppliers and,
65–67
management of outsourcing
contract and, 67–69,
97–98
selective approach and, 60,
69–70
sourcing decision at, 61–65
enterprise resource planning
(ERP) systems, 161
enterprise systems
attractions of, 160, 164–167
automated processes and,
135–138, 178
configuration of, 183–185
creation of, 141–145
customization and, 168,
169–170, 183–185
design of intelligent corporation and, 145–151
Elf Atochem and, 176–181
guidelines for managing by
wire and, 151–156
impacts on organization,
171–176
as maps, 143
risks in, 150–151, 159–160,
161–162, 164, 167–171
scope of, 162, 163
structure of, 166
tools in, 143–145
Y2K remediation and,
210–212
Ernst & Young, 123, 124, 126,
202
ERP systems. *See* enterprise
resource planning

systems
European antitrust law, 95
European Union, and Y2K, 189

Federal Aviation Administration (FAA), 189
federalist operating model, 174–175
Fields, Debbi, 136. *See also* Mrs. Fields Cookies
Fields, Randy, 136
financial records, and Y2K, 199
financial services industry, 190–191, 214, 215
First Fidelity Bancorp, 109
Fitzgerald, Guy, 75
flexibility, 132
  institutionalization of, 138–141
  IT outsourcing and, 59, 84, 88–89, 103, 113, 115–116
flying by wire, 131–132, 134, 152
FoxMeyer Drug, 161

Gemini Sogeti. *See* Hoskyns Group
general manager. *See also* line managers; manage-by-wire system
  enterprise systems and, 181–183
  role in IT function and, 40–42
Gillotti, Deborah, 210–212
Global Insurance (fictional company name),

148–151, 152, 154, 156
GPM Gas Corporation, 36, 40–43
Granada Computer Services, 87
Grossman, Jerome H., 54–56
groupware, 26–29

Hallmark Cards, 24–25
Hands On Network Environment (HONE), 30–32
Harvard Business School, 207
Harvard Pilgrim Health Care, 205
health care industry. *See* New England Medical Center
Hewlett-Packard, 174, 175–176
Hiner, Glen, 173–174
HONE. *See* Hands On Network Environment
Hoskyns Group, 87
Huber, Dick, 107
human-centered approach
  information culture and, 4, 20–29
  information facts of life and, 29–30
  information sharing and, 13–20
  multiple meanings and, 3–4, 8–13
  traditional IT and, 5–8

IBM, 59. *See also* Integrated Systems Solutions Corporation
  "information architecture" and, 6

IBM (*continued*)
  information maps and,
    23–24, 30–32
  Storage Systems division,
    167
  Y2K problem and, 190
industry alliances, and Y2K
  problem, 214
I-Net, 102, 103
inevitability, and Y2K problem,
  207–210
information architecture
  concept of, 6
  human-centered approach
    and, 9
  integration of, 113, 127, 137,
    159, 160 (*See also* enter-
    prise systems)
information culture
  human-centered approach
    and, 4, 16, 20–29
  outsourcing of IT and, 90
information facts of life, 29–30
information globalism versus
  information particular-
  ism, 11–12
information guides, 24–25
information maps, 23–24, 203.
  See also enterprise systems
information sharing models.
  See also enterprise systems
  assumptions about, 4
  problems with, 13–120
information technology (IT)
  knowledge of, and outsourc-

ing decision, 74–75
  proprietary technology and,
    115
  technological change and,
    48, 73, 80–81, 101,
    112–113
information technology (IT)
  departments
  as intermediary between
    policy and execution,
    140–141
  internal consulting and,
    103–105
  management of, 40–43, 86
  role of, with outsourced IT,
    85–87
  Y2K problem and, 192
information technology (IT)
  investments. *See also*
    manage-by-wire system;
    outsourcing of IT
  appropriateness of technol-
    ogy and, 38–39, 54
  and business considera-
    tions, 41–42, 46–47, 84,
    128, 176
  follow-on commitments
    and, 38
  integrated capabilities and,
    51–53, 55, 132, 159, 160
  sourcing decision at BP and,
    87–89
  team approach to, 53–54
information technology (IT)
  service suppliers
  choice of, 65–67, 93–99
  conflicts among, 100–101

multiple supplier strategy
and, 86–87, 88–89, 93–99,
100–101
outsourcing contracts with,
67–69, 75–80, 97–99,
124–125
supplier capabilities and,
90–93
institutional learning, 146–151
Integrated Systems Solutions
Corporation (ISSC), 108,
123, 125–127
inventories, and Y2K problem,
198
ISSC. *See* Integrated Systems
Solutions Corporation
IT. *See entries at information
technology*

Japanese steel industry, 116

language of business design,
154
learning loop, 146–151
line managers, 37, 42, 43, 45,
49. *See also* general manager
litigation, and Y2K, 190,
216–219
Lotus Notes, 17, 26–29

McGraw-Hill, 155
McKinsey & Company, 197
manage-by-wire system. *See
also* enterprise systems
at Brooklyn Union, 138–141
corporate IQ and, 141–142

creation of enterprise model
and, 141–145
design of intelligent corporation and, 145–151
guidelines for, 151–156
ideal implementation of,
134
"managing by wire" as term,
132–134
at Mrs. Fields, 135–138
pace of implementation of,
155–156
management discussion and
analysis (MD&A), 202
Manufacturers Hanover, 14–16
Martin, Bob L., 35, 37–40
Massachusetts Institute of
Technology (MIT), Sloan
School of Management,
47–50
MD&A. *See* management discussion and analysis
Medical Center Information
Services Advisory
Committee (New Eng-
land Medical Center),
55–56
Merck. *See* Astra Merck
mergers, and information sharing, 14–16
Milan, Thomas, 202–205
MIT. *See* Massachusetts Insti-
tute of Technology, Sloan
School of Management
Mobil Europe, 161
modules, in enterprise systems,
183–184

Monsanto, 174, 175–176
Mrs. Fields Cookies, 135–138,
    142
multinational corporations,
    and enterprise systems,
    173–174
multiple meanings, and
    human-centered
    approach, 3–4, 8–13

NCR Cooperation groupware,
    26
negotiation of outsourcing
    contracts, 77–78, 97–98,
    102, 124–125
Nestlé, 174
networks, IT-enabled, 139
Newcomb, Jonathan, 36, 43–47
New England Medical Center,
    54–56
noninformation versus infor-
    mation, 17–18

object-oriented programming,
    140, 141, 149. *See also*
    manage-by-wire system
OODA Loop, 146, 147
organizational capabilities
    integration of IT with,
        51–53, 55, 132
    technology investments
        and, 36
    theory of business and,
        47–50
organizational structure
    enterprise systems and,
        171–176, 178–179

integration of IT in, 52–54,
    139
IT investment decisions
    and, 55–56
IT outsourcing decision
    and, 118
Otis Elevator, 14
outsourcing of IT
    at British Petroleum, 83–105
    choice of suppliers and,
        65–67, 93–99, 120–125
    at Continental Bank,
        107–129
    decision to outsource and,
        113–117
    framework for decisions on,
        72–81
    implementation challenges
        and, 99–105, 117–120
    internal IT departments
        and, 89–90, 103–105,
        122–123
    lessons on technology
        alliances and, 128–129
    multiple supplier strategy
        and, 85–87, 88–89, 93–99,
        100–101
    outsourcing contracts and,
        67–69, 75–80, 97–99,
        124–125
    pricing and, 123–124
    requests for proposals,
        121–122
    results of, 70–72, 125–128
    selective approach to, 60,
        69–72, 85–86, 87–89
    strategic-versus-commodity

approach to, 58–59,
62–65
supplier capabilities and,
90–93, 121–122

Penn Square Bank, 107, 108
Perot Systems, 60
pharmaceutical industry. *See*
Astra Merck
planning. *See also* Year 2000
problem
early, and Y2K problem, 199
enterprise systems and, 179
pricing, and IT outsourcing,
123–124
process control
enterprise systems and,
135–138, 178
Y2K problem and, 199,
210–212
public perceptions, and Y2K
problem, 206–207, 215
public utilities industry. *See*
Brooklyn Union Gas of
New York

Quotron, 114

Radin, Stephen A., 216–219
Rank Xerox, U.K., 7–8
recruiting, and Y2K, 201
red shift, 154
retail book industry. *See*
Simon & Schuster
Retail Operations Intelligence
(ROI) system, 138
risk

CEO IT decisions and, 35, 37
enterprise systems and,
150–151, 159–160,
161–162, 164, 167–171
risk-and-mitigation plans,
and Y2K, 202, 203,
205–207
Robbins, Brian, 219–222
Rockart, John F., 47–50
"Rumor Mill," 17

SAIC. *See* Science Applications
International Corpora-
tion
SAP, 161, 168–169, 175, 177,
178
Science Applications International Corporation
(SAIC), 94–96, 97, 99, 103
Securities and Exchange Commission (SEC), 202, 204,
219
Sema Group, 94–96, 99
senior management, and IT
knowledge, 73–74,
215–216. *See also* chief
executive officer; chief
information officer; gen-
eral manager
sewage-control plant, and Y2K,
189
shareholder derivative suits,
216–217
shareholder litigation, 216–219
sharing, and corporate IQ, 142,
153
Sheinheit, Steve, 219–222

Simon & Schuster, 36, 43–47
solution integrators, 52. *See
    also* systems integrators
Spar, Jeffrey, 197–202
specialists, and outsourcing
    contracts, 77–78
Spong, Stephanie, 197–202
Spright, Debra, 205–207
Starbucks Coffee Company,
    210
stirrup, 208–209
strategic systems, and IT out-
    sourcing, 58–59, 62–65,
    72–73
Strauss, Norman, 202–205
structuring, and corporate IQ,
    142, 153–154
subcontracting, outsourcing
    suppliers and, 98
Symantec Corporation, 19
Syncordia, 94–96, 97, 98, 99
systems integrators, 79–80. *See
    also* solution integrators

Tandem Computers, 18
task force. *See* teams
teams
    changing technology and,
        80–81
    enterprise system imple-
        mentation and, 180–181
    investment decisions and,
        53–54, 55–56
    IT leadership and, 42–43
    outsourcing decisions and,
        62–65, 66, 91–92,

118–120, 126
outsourcing management
    and, 78–79, 125–128
technical council at Continen-
    tal Bank, 118–120
technical oversight group
    (TOG), 126
technological change
    IT management and, 48, 73,
        80–81, 101, 112–113
    unintended consequences
        of, 208–209
technology suppliers, as source
    of information, 39, 75.
    See also information
    technology service
    suppliers
Tedlow, Richard S., 207–210
Theobald, Tom, 111
"theory of business," 47
TOG. *See* technical oversight
    group

uncertainty
    IT outsourcing decisions
        and, 63
    Y2K problem and, 192, 197,
        203, 204
Union Carbide, 172
Union Pacific Railroad, 10
United Kingdom, Royal Mail,
    73
U. S. Air Force. *See* OODA
    Loop
U. S. Department of Agricul-
    ture, 10

value creation, and coordination of business units,
155
Vanguard Group, 193
vision, and IT use, 49

Wall Street Journal, 189
Wal-Mart Stores, 35, 37–40,
147–148, 154
Weil, Gotshal & Manges, 216
White, Lynn, Jr., 208–209
Willcocks, Leslie, 75

Xerox Corporation, 12–13,
16–17

Yardeni, Edward, 212–216
Year 2000 (Y2K) problem
benefits of planning for,
196–197
communication and,
194–195, 202–205,
206–207, 219, 222
defensive strategy for,
195–196

economic impact of,
191–192, 206
enterprise systems and, 181
external threats and,
189–190, 195–196,
197–202, 212–216, 221
functions outside of IS
domain and, 210–212
internal systems and,
193–195, 205–206, 220
litigation and, 190, 216–219
notion of inevitability and,
207–210
offensive strategy for,
193–195
as opportunity, 200–201,
221–222
pervasiveness of, 187–188
preparation for disruption
and, 212–216, 219–222
risk-and-mitigation plans
and, 202, 203, 205–207
Yetter, Wayne P., 36, 50–54
Y2K problem. *See* Year 2000
problem

NATIONWIDE LIBRARY